How to Cook
for Beginners

GWYN NOVAK

How to Cook

for BEGINNERS

An Easy Cookbook for
Learning the Basics

ROCKRIDGE
PRESS

For general information on our other products and services or to obtain technical support, please contact our Customer Care Department within the United States at (866) 744-2665, or outside the United States at (510) 253-0500.

Rockridge Press publishes its books in a variety of electronic and print formats. Some content that appears in print may not be available in electronic books, and vice versa.

TRADEMARKS: Rockridge Press and the Rockridge Press logo are trademarks or registered trademarks of Callisto Media Inc. and/or its affiliates, in the United States and other countries, and may not be used without written permission. All other trademarks are the property of their respective owners. Rockridge Press is not associated with any product or vendor mentioned in this book.

Interior and Cover Designer: John Calmeyer
Art Producer: Sue Bischofberger
Editors: Sam Eichner and Lauren Ladoceour
Production Manager: Martin Worthington
Production Editor: Kurt Shulenberger

Illustrations: © 2019 Tom Bingham.

Photography: © Shannon Douglas, pp. xii, 156; © Marija Vidal, pp. 10, 52, 112, 120, 152; © Darren Muir, pp. 22, 32, 39, 64, 72, 74, 81, 90, 104, 116, 128, 130, 142, 144; © Hélène Dujardin, pp. 26, 40, 44, 68, 114, 134, 138; © Nadine Greeff, pp. 30, 54, 60, 70, 110, 158, 160; © Evi Abeler, pp. 42, 149, 150; © zkruger/iStock, p. 46; © Michele Olivier, p, 50; © mphillips007/iStock, p. 56; © C+N Creative, p. 58; © ola_p/iStock, p. 82; © Melina Hammer, pp. 92, 98, 126; © Jennifer Davick, p. 100.

ISBN: Print 978-1-64152-931-0
eBook 978-1-64152-932-7

R0

To all the amazing women cooks in my life.

Table of Contents

Introduction

Welcome to the flavorful world of cooking! Whether you're devoted to takeout or still wondering how to boil water, I promise you this: You can cook. No one is born knowing how to make delicious food, and it's never too late to learn. Even the great Julia Child didn't get started until she was in her forties.

Growing up in southern Maryland, just outside Washington, D.C., I was surrounded by some really fabulous cooks. My Grandmother McKenney ran a well-known seafood restaurant on Solomons Island, where I spent summers in the kitchen watching her staff cook. My mother, a home economics teacher for 31 years, taught just about every middle schooler in the area how to bake cookies.

Oh, I was happy enough to enjoy the fruits of their labor. But as a twentysomething, I had absolutely no interest in making food for myself at home. I was busy pursuing a career in international politics. It wasn't until I was in graduate school—working at a kitchen store to pay the rent—that something changed. To escape the stress of my classes, I found refuge in the kitchen. It started with all-day marathons of PBS cooking shows (in the days before Food Network) and experimenting with easy recipes—roasted chicken, creamy mashed potatoes, and chocolate mousse. Cooking and eating meals I made myself became my passion. In less than a semester, it was bye-bye, grad school; hello, cooking school!

I tell you all of this to say this book is truly designed for the beginner cook.

I'll start by walking you through everything you need to know to create simple, tasty meals for you and your family and friends. In part 1, I will help you get started outfitting your kitchen with the essential equipment, show you how to take care of your knives, and detail the contents of a well-equipped pantry.

In part 2, we'll move on to basic cooking techniques, such as knife skills, boiling, pan cooking, and baking; at the end of each section, you will create a recipe utilizing the technique you just learned. And finally, in part 3, it all comes together with a variety of easy recipes to add to your personal repertoire.

I know that learning anything new can seem challenging at first. But, as I tell my students, cooking isn't rocket science. It should be fun. So, relax and enjoy it. Experiment with different ingredients and seasonings. Soak in the aromas, colors, and flavors. Let them linger on your senses. Food is about so much more than just feeding our bellies. It's really about feeding our souls. Most importantly, it's meant to be shared with family and friends. Kudos to you for having the courage to learn a new skill. Now let's get cooking!

PART ONE

Getting Started

CHAPTER ONE

Welcome to Your Kitchen

In this chapter, we're going to get you ready to cook. We'll cover basic rules and the equipment you need to make your life easier and more enjoyable in the kitchen.

Why Bother to Cook?

I'm a firm believer that if you eat (and I know you do!), you really should learn to cook. Don't get me wrong, eating out is great—I'm the first one to enjoy a good dinner at one of my favorite restaurants—but a steady diet of fast food, takeout, and processed foods can be tough on your wallet and your waistline. Did you know you can typically prepare a healthy, delicious meal in less time than it takes for delivery to show up? You'll not only save money by cooking your own food; you'll also see major health benefits. And there's nothing better than the *oohs* and *aahs* you'll get from family and friends when you serve their favorite meal, made entirely from scratch.

GOLDEN RULES

To prepare a delicious meal, it's helpful to follow a few general guidelines to make sure cooking is successful and stress-free.

1 Read the entire recipe at least once before you begin cooking. It really helps to know how the recipe is going to progress before you get started and that you have everything you need to make the recipe.

2 Have all your ingredients ready to go. Professional kitchens call this *mise en place*—everything in its place. This way, you won't get partway through the recipe and realize you're missing something.

3 Keep it simple and uncluttered. Simpler recipes are often the best, and it's always easier and less stressful to work in a clean, uncluttered kitchen.

4 Practice, practice, practice. Find a few recipes you really like and make them a few times to get really comfortable. Then show them off to family and friends.

5 Focus. Really hone in on what you're doing when you are cooking. Distractions can mean missed ingredients as well as under- or overcooked foods.

6 Be patient. You've heard the saying, "Good food takes time." Set aside ample time to make a recipe, and give yourself a few extra minutes—just in case. An additional minute or two can mean the difference between a mediocre meal and an exceptional one.

7 Trust your instincts. Just because a recipe says it needs only a pinch of salt doesn't always mean that it's so. If it tastes like it's missing a little something extra, by all means, go for it.

ESSENTIAL GEAR

Having the right equipment makes all the difference in the kitchen. The following are the must-haves to gather before you start.

10-Inch Nonstick Sauté Pan or Skillet This pan will be your go-to for dinner most nights, as it will make cooking and cleanup much easier.

Baking Pans It's helpful to have baking pans of various sizes—a loaf pan for meatloaf and quick breads, an 8-by-8-inch pan for small cakes, and a muffin tin for various sweet and savory recipes.

Baking Sheets and Sheet Pans When choosing baking sheets, make sure they are not flimsy (or your food will burn). They also need to fit in your oven, but you don't want them so small that you have to use multiple pans. Have at least one rimless baking sheet and one rimmed sheet pan.

Box Grater This is a four-sided metal box with variously sized holes for grating.

Can Opener Get a heavy-duty hand-held can opener. It will store easily in a drawer.

Cast-Iron Enamel-Covered Pot with Lid (Dutch Oven) From making bread to soups and stews, this multi-use pot will become one of your favorites.

Cast-Iron Skillet Cast-iron pans have seen a resurgence in the past few years. Vintage pans go for hundreds of dollars on eBay. But you can find one at any kitchen supply store or a secondhand shop for much less, and you might even have one collecting dust in your basement. Cast-iron pans last forever if properly cared for and are especially great for cooking meats on the stovetop or for meals that require you to transfer a pan to the oven.

Colander Look for a nice, wide colander. A metal colander can also double as a steamer basket.

Cookie Scoop A tablespoon-size scoop is perfect for portioning out cookie dough and ice cream.

Cutting Boards Choose a beautiful wooden board that fits your kitchen space and décor. But beyond that, have a few flexible plastic boards stashed in the pantry. I never cut raw meat on my wooden board. Save that for the plastic to prevent cross-contamination. A flexible plastic cutting board is also great for diced veggies. Just pick the whole thing up and take it straight to the pan!

Good, Sharp Knives and Kitchen Shears Forget those cheap "bargain" knife sets—all you need is an 8-inch chef's knife, a paring knife, and a serrated knife, plus a pair of kitchen shears. These will get you through just about anything you'll do in the kitchen. And here's a pro tip: The Victorinox Fibrox line of knives is used in many professional kitchens and is ridiculously affordable. You don't have to spend a fortune to get a great knife.

Fish Spatula Forget the traditional flat metal spatula; opt for an angled fish spatula. It is so much easier to get food (not just fish) out of a pan when using this tool. It's also a good idea to have a plastic spatula to use on your nonstick pans so you don't scratch them.

Instant-Read Thermometer Get a thermometer with a digital readout; it's so much easier to see. You'll use this for chicken, beef, and pork to make sure they're cooked to the proper temperature.

Large Spoons (Metal, Slotted, and Wooden) You need a metal spoon for stirring and a slotted spoon for removing foods from the pan. Wooden spoons are great for deglazing (see page 85) as well as stirring just about anything.

Measuring Cups and Spoons (Dry and Liquid) Choose heavy-duty dry measuring cups and spoons that don't bend easily. Look for liquid measuring cups with measurement marks you can read from above. No more stooping over to read amounts. I know this seems silly, but trust me—you're going to love them!

Mixing Bowls Get a set of different-sized mixing bowls—preferably metal or plastic. Lids are a bonus.

Mixer (Stand and Handheld) A standing mixer is a heavy-duty piece of equipment that is perfect if you cook or bake a great deal. You can place ingredients in the bowl and walk away while it mixes. A handheld electric mixer stores easily in a drawer and is great to have around for smaller tasks. But unlike a standing mixer, you can't walk away from it while it's mixing.

Oven Mitts Get at least two.

Pastry Brush Resembling a small paintbrush, a pastry brush is perfect for applying egg wash or butter onto pastry dough or other foods.

Roasting Pan with a Rack A sturdy metal roasting pan is great for larger foods; its accompanying metal rack sits inside the roasting pan, keeping the food from touching the bottom of the pan so heat circulates around it more evenly.

Rubber Spatulas Rubber spatulas, particularly the curved kind, are perfect for getting every last bit out of a bowl or pan. The silicone kind is heat resistant, too.

Tongs Invest in two pairs of metal tongs. Be sure they have rubber on the handles—not the tips! Food slides off of rubber tips, making it much harder to pick the food up.

Vegetable Peeler Invest in a good-quality Y-shaped peeler. It's quicker and easier to use than a straight peeler.

Wire Cooling Rack These are perfect for channeling airflow around cookies, cakes, and other baked goods as they cool.

HOW TO CARE FOR KNIVES

Now that you have a few great knives, you're going to have to take care of them. This means storing them properly so they maintain their sharp edge and having them sharpened periodically. Regardless of how good any knife is, it will dull with regular use. Let's start with storing them.

I like to keep my knives in a wooden knife block. Others prefer to hang them from a magnetic strip. Either way is fine. It's all about personal preference. Whatever you do, do not store them in a drawer where they can knock into other utensils. Regular contact made against the blade (particularly with other metal utensils) will quickly dull your knives.

One of the best ways to keep your knives in good shape and maintain the cutting edge between sharpenings is to run them across a honing steel (sometimes erroneously called a sharpening steel) every week or so. A honing steel is a long metal rod with a handle. You simply place the heel of the knife blade (the part of the knife's edge closest to the handle) against the tip of the steel at about a 20-degree angle and pull the blade across the steel in a sweeping motion so the tip of the blade ends up touching the handle of the steel, while maintaining that 20-degree angle. Repeat on each side (alternating after each pull—front, back, front, back) 5 to 10 times, always maintaining the 20-degree angle while you pull across the entire length of the blade. This aligns the blade and hones it to keep the cutting edge straight and sharp.

Every few months, you might begin to sense that the steel just isn't giving your knives the sharpness you want. That's when you need to put a new edge on the blade, and I suggest you have that done professionally. You can learn how to do this yourself using whetstones, but for about $5 per knife, it's worth it to find a local knifesmith who really knows what they're doing. If you do it yourself, you risk taking away more of the blade than you intended.

You'll know it's time for a sharpening when your knife doesn't easily cut through foods like it used to. If you have to push down too hard or tear through the food, those are good indications it's time to have your knife sharpened. And remember: A sharp knife is a safer knife.

Grocery Shopping

Having all the necessary ingredients on hand makes cooking so much more enjoyable, but it also requires a thoughtful visit to the grocery store. Ideally, you want to limit your trips to once a week, or it becomes a lot of extra work and time. Start by making a master grocery list of all the ingredients you will need that week to prepare the recipes you have chosen. Go through each recipe and add the ingredients to your list. I like to break down my list by categories: produce, meats, dairy, frozen, cleaning supplies, pantry items, and so on. Organizing your grocery list makes it easier and quicker to shop once you're in the store. I even arrange my grocery list according to the layout of the store. In other words, if produce is the first section you come to, list produce first on your grocery list.

QUICK TIP: Save refrigerated and frozen foods for your last stop before the checkout so they will stay colder longer.

PANTRY STAPLES

Good cooks start with the essentials—this means keeping a well-stocked pantry, fridge, and freezer. Who wants to have to run to the store every time you make a meal? You don't need to get all these things, but it wouldn't hurt when you're first starting out. With a well-stocked kitchen, you might even find that on occasion, you'll have everything you need to make dinner without even having to buy groceries. And who doesn't love that? What follows is a list of must-haves for your pantry:

- All-purpose flour, preferably unbleached

- Black pepper

- Bread crumbs, preferably the panko (Japanese-style) variety

- Canned broths (reduced-sodium chicken and vegetable)

- Canned beans (black beans, cannellini beans, chickpeas)

- Canned diced tomatoes

- Garlic (whole heads)

- Honey

- Nonstick cooking spray

- Nuts (almonds, pecans, pine nuts, walnuts)
- Oils (canola, soybean, and extra-virgin olive oils)
- Onions (yellow and red)
- Pasta (regular or whole grain)—choose spaghetti or linguine, and shells or penne
- Potatoes (russet, Yukon Gold)
- Salt (kosher and sea salt)
- Tomato sauce
- Vinegar (red and white wine vinegar, balsamic vinegar, apple cider vinegar)
- Rice (brown and white)
- Sugar (granulated and brown)

Dried Herbs and Spices

- Basil
- Bay leaves
- Cayenne pepper
- Chili powder
- Cinnamon
- Cumin
- Curry powder
- Garlic powder
- Oregano
- Rosemary
- Thyme

FRESH INGREDIENTS

Just like you did with the pantry, stock your refrigerator with the following fresh ingredients to make cooking a breeze.

- Bacon
- Barbecue sauce
- Butter (salted or unsalted)
- Cheeses (Cheddar, goat, mozzarella, Parmesan)
- Dijon mustard
- Eggs
- Ketchup
- Lemons
- Mayonnaise
- Milk and half-and-half
- Salsa
- Sour cream

HOW LONG FOOD LASTS

Food labels can be a little confusing between sell-by, use-by, and expiration dates. What do they all mean?

Sell-By Date: This is the date after which the grocery store will remove the item from its shelf. It is still safe to eat for about one week from that date.

Use-By Date: After this date, the product begins to lose its freshness. It's still safe to eat; it just won't be at its peak.

Expiration Date: Throw it away after this date. It's no longer safe to eat.

Remember—rely on your senses. If it looks, smells, or tastes funny, throw it away!

There are few things more frustrating than spending a lot of money on food only to have it go bad and end up in the trash. The best way to avoid throwing away money is to purchase fresh ingredients in smaller amounts and use them quickly.

Proper storage of fresh items unquestionably helps prolong their life span. Be sure to put vegetables in the crisper drawers of your refrigerator. When you get home from the market, take veggies out of plastic bags (plastic speeds up their decay). Dairy products are best stored in the coldest part of the refrigerator.

When it comes to leftovers, label them so you know exactly what they are later on. Use a permanent marker to indicate what's inside and the date you cooked it.

QUICK TIP: Never store eggs in the refrigerator door, because they warm up every time the door is opened.

CHAPTER TWO

Best Practices

Before you dive into cooking, set yourself up for success by learning what most good cooks consider the basics: safety tips for the kitchen, how to read a recipe, and how to properly season food. We'll cover all that and more in this chapter to get you cooking like a "seasoned" pro.

Reading a Recipe

Recipes are detailed road maps for how to create a finished dish. Each recipe in this book tells you how many people it serves or how much it makes (the "yield"). It also includes the amount of time it takes to prepare (the "prep time") and the "cook time," which is how long you will actually spend cooking the recipe.

A good recipe always includes a list of measured ingredients. Sometimes measurements are spelled out, as in this book, but often the units of measure are abbreviated. Here is a quick list of common culinary abbreviations:

lb = pound   tbsp = tablespoon

tsp = teaspoon   oz = ounce

The ingredients are typically listed in the order in which they are used in the recipe so you don't have to search for what you need next.

Following the list of ingredients are the directions to prepare the recipe. It's really important to read the entire recipe at least once before you start cooking, so you know what to expect.

Prep a Workstation

Cooking can be very relaxing in the right environment—meaning one free of clutter and chaos. No one can create amazing meals in a kitchen full of dirty dishes and food left out on the counter. So before you even begin to cook, clean up and give yourself plenty of counter space on which to work.

Also, make sure your equipment is clean and close at hand. For many cooks, this means having a good cutting board in front of you. Be sure to secure it in place so it doesn't slide on the counter—that's a sure way to cut yourself. The easiest way to secure the board is to place a damp paper towel underneath it. Like magic, there will be no sliding.

I also like to keep a trash can or a bowl for scraps nearby so I can clean as I go.

And finally, it's a good idea to have a kitchen towel or two close by as well as a roll of paper towels for spills and wiping your hands.

CLEAN UP—BEFORE, DURING, AND AFTER

Just as you cleaned up before you started cooking, carry that strategy through the entire recipe. Dishes, trash, and food piling up around you as you cook can be very stressful, and no one likes to get to the end of dinner and see a mountain of dishes, pots, and pans in the sink. So clean as you go. Not only will it mean a calmer kitchen to work in, but it will also be safer. Keep your cutting board and the surrounding area clear of excess ingredients. With more room to work, your chances of cutting yourself are greatly reduced.

COOKING LINGO

Cooking has its own language. Words get thrown around with the assumption that everyone knows what they mean: *season to taste, caramelize, deglaze*. The following glossary of common cooking terms will remove the guesswork for you.

Al dente: This is an Italian phrase meaning "to the tooth." When pasta is properly cooked, it still has a little bite or "tooth"—it's not mushy.

Brown/caramelize: To cook meat or vegetables over high heat until it browns on the exterior; if the food contains natural sugars, such as carrots or sweet potatoes, that sugar caramelizes, or browns, too.

Cream: To blend butter and sugar together until it becomes a light and creamy mixture.

Cross-contamination: When potentially harmful bacteria from uncooked meats are spread from one surface to another.

Deglaze: To add liquid to a pan to loosen the stuck, cooked-on pieces from the bottom. This technique is usually used to make pan sauces.

Dice: To cut food into small, uniform cubes.

High heat/sear: Intense stovetop heat that cooks food very quickly.

Low heat: A gentle heat that just warms the food.

Medium-high heat: Heat set on a stovetop burner that is slightly hotter than medium but not so hot that the pan smokes or burns.

Mince: To cut food into very small pieces.

Prep: To prepare ingredients or equipment as a recipe directs before using them, such as greasing a pan or chopping carrots.

Rest: To let meat sit after cooking (off the heat or out of the oven) for about 10 minutes to reabsorb the juices, which produces a more tender and moist dish.

Season to taste: To add spices, such as salt and pepper, to enhance the natural flavor of the food, using your own discretion as to how much is enough.

Truss: To tie together the legs of a chicken (or other type of poultry) with kitchen twine so it cooks more evenly.

Zest: To grate the outer skin of a citrus fruit for flavor using a zester, or the grated skin itself.

Keeping Safe in the Kitchen

When it comes to kitchen safety, incidents tend to fall into one of three categories: kitchen fires, sharp objects, and harmful bacteria. What follows are some key safety tips to keep in mind as you work more regularly in your kitchen.

KITCHEN FIRES

Most kitchen fires are a result of grease or oil that gets too hot. To avoid this, know that the first sign a pan is getting too hot is that it will start to smoke. Eventually, if left unattended, it will catch fire. If you see a pan begin to smoke, immediately remove it from the heat and cover it if you can. Make sure you wear an oven mitt when moving the pan.

Keep a fully charged fire extinguisher in the kitchen in the event of fire. Make sure it is rated to put out a grease fire.

In the event you do not have a fire extinguisher, you can put out a small kitchen fire by covering it with a pot lid or sprinkling it liberally with baking soda. Never cover a pan fire with a kitchen towel or pour water on the fire. That will make the fire worse.

SHARP OBJECTS

Believe it or not, a dull knife is more dangerous than a sharp knife. Dull knives require you to pull or push too hard, which can result in a nasty cut. To prevent other unwanted cuts, never put knives in the dishwasher or a kitchen sink full of soapy, bubbly water that hides sharp objects.

But knives aren't the only sharp blades to be cautious of—think blenders, food processors, and vegetable peelers. Take your time when handling, washing, drying, and storing these items to prevent cuts.

HARMFUL BACTERIA

Be careful how you handle raw meats and seafood, as they contain harmful bacteria. Keep a dedicated, separate plastic or acrylic cutting board for raw meats. Wash the board, along with any utensils and bowls used for raw meat, in hot, soapy water immediately after use, and let it completely dry before using it again. Be sure to wash your hands thoroughly before touching anything else to prevent spreading harmful bacteria. To prevent cross-contamination, do not put cooked meats back on the same plate you used when they were raw.

Some foods, such as chicken, must be thoroughly cooked to kill all the bacteria. If you cut into cooked beef or pork, a pink interior and minimum temperature of 145°F is considered safe—but the same isn't true for chicken. Make sure chicken is cooked to an internal temperature of 165°F (which you can check with an instant-read thermometer).

Cooking with Heat

When you're cooking indoors, there are two basic methods: You can use your stovetop or your oven. Stovetop cooking is exactly what the name implies. All the cooking is done on the burners on top of the stove, whereas oven cooking takes place—you guessed it—inside the oven.

Each stove and oven is a bit different; therefore, it's a good idea to consult the appliance's user manual for detailed directions. Regardless of whether you have a gas or electric stove and oven, the following guidelines apply.

KEYS TO COOKING ON YOUR STOVE

Keep these tips in mind when you're using your stovetop. They'll help you maximize your time, stay safe, and generally improve your cooking experience.

Use burners about the same size as your pan. This results in faster, more even cooking and wastes less energy.

Keep the pan's handle facing inward. Handles that face out (away from the stove) are easy to accidently hit, resulting in a spill. Be careful, though, that they're not over another hot burner.

Don't use metal utensils in a nonstick pan. They will scratch the pan, thereby removing the nonstick surface.

Don't leave utensils in the pan or pot. Metal utensils will get very hot, and plastic might melt.

Keep kitchen towels away from all stovetops. They can easily catch on fire.

Turn on the exhaust fan. If you're cooking with a lot of oil or high heat, turn on the exhaust fan to clear any smoke.

Use oven mitts to move pots and pans. Pots and pans can heat up quickly, particularly those with metal handles. Be careful when moving them.

Never use a wet or damp towel or oven mitt on a hot pot. Use a dry oven mitt instead. The damp item will create steam when it touches the hot pot, resulting in a painful burn.

KEYS TO COOKING WITH YOUR OVEN

Using these easy tips will go a long way when it comes to cooking with your oven.

Always preheat your oven. Unless the recipe states otherwise, preheat your oven before you put food inside. Food cooks faster and more evenly when the oven is preheated.

Bake versus broil. The Bake setting, which will be used for most of your cooking, surrounds the food with hot air. Broiling heats the food from the top only and uses a very high, intense heat that is great for quickly browning foods in the oven.

The ideal place to cook in the oven is in its center. If you can, choose the center of the middle rack. You'll typically have the most even heat in this spot, but do note that many ovens have "hot spots," and you may have to use some trial and error to locate them.

Use a timer. We all think we're going to remember to take the food out of the oven at the right time, but life is distracting. Set it and forget it—until you're reminded!

Use oven mitts. The food will be hot when it comes out of the oven. Use oven mitts to protect your hands.

Stand away from the open door. A rush of hot air is going to escape the oven when you open the door. Do yourself a favor and stand back to let it pass before you remove the food from the oven.

HOW TO KNOW WHEN IT'S READY TO EAT

In part 2, we will go into greater detail on cooking times and cues, as different foods have different degrees of doneness. But the table below contains general rules of thumb for recognizing doneness.

FOOD	WHEN IT'S DONE
Beans	The beans will be softened but not mushy.
Beef	Depending on your preference, the internal temperature will be as follows. Rare: 125°F to 135°F; medium-rare: 145°F; medium: 160°F; medium-well: 165°F; well-done: 170°F. Note that the minimum temperature recommended by the U.S. Department of Agriculture is 145°F for cuts of beef and 160° for ground beef, and these are all temperatures before a resting period.
Bread	It sounds hollow when you tap it.
Cake	A toothpick inserted into the center comes out clean, with no raw batter attached.
Chicken and other poultry	The internal temperature is 165°F, measured with an instant-read thermometer in the deepest part of the meat (and not touching bone); the juices will run clear when pierced.
Cookies	Cookie edges are lightly browned.
Eggs	If fried, yolk is runny, white is firm; if hardboiled, yolk and white are firm.
Fish	The flesh is firm to the touch and not translucent.
Grains	All the water is absorbed; grains are not hard but not too soft.
Pasta	The pasta is al dente—with a bit of texture but not too soft.
Pork	For whole cuts, the internal temperature is 145°F; for ground pork, 160°F.
Rice	It is not crunchy and not too soft. Similar to pasta, rice should be cooked al dente.
Sausage	The internal temperature is 165°F; there should be no pink inside (unless it is a specific style of sausage).
Vegetables	They are tender but not mushy; this is sometimes called "fork-tender" or "crisp-tender."

Seasoning to Taste

One of the things I see students struggle with the most in my classes is how to properly season food. Underseasoned food is bland and unappetizing, which is precisely why this is an important technique to master. It will take time and practice. There's no hard-and-fast rule for how much seasoning to add to a dish. You just need to practice and taste your food. But the three basic ingredients to master when it comes to flavoring your food are salt, pepper, and fat.

SALT

Salt is the most important ingredient in cooking. It is a natural flavor enhancer and, when added in the proper proportions, brings food to life. You often read recipes that tell you to "season to taste." But what does that phrase mean? Essentially, it means to add enough salt (and pepper) to bring out the flavors of your food. Go slowly and gradually, tasting as you go. Add a bit of salt and taste your dish. If it seems a bit bland, add more, stopping short of making it too salty. If it tastes like the ocean, you've added too much.

PEPPER

When a recipe calls for pepper, it means black pepper unless otherwise specified. Black pepper brings a little bit of spiciness to a dish. It really helps round out the flavors. I always use whole black peppercorns and grind them myself. Pepper grinders are relatively inexpensive, and the flavor of freshly ground pepper is so much better than the preground, often powdery store-bought versions. Another advantage is that you can change the coarseness of the grind when you grind it yourself.

FAT

Fat is second only to salt when it comes to adding flavor to a dish. *Fat* typically means oil (olive oil, vegetable or soy oil, canola oil, and coconut oil are some typical choices) or butter. While these can often be used interchangeably, each brings its own flavors and benefits to the table. Butter is rich in full-bodied flavor, but it has a lower smoke point, which means it isn't the best choice when you're cooking with high heat. Most oils, on the other hand, are a bit lighter in flavor and can take a higher heat. But if you want, say, a great brown on pan-seared chicken, a combination of the two is best.

About the Techniques and Recipes

Congratulations! You made it through the first section. Now you're ready to start cooking! In part 2, you'll learn specific techniques vital to learning to cook. From proper measuring and knife skills to sautéing and baking, each skill builds on the next to increase your confidence in the kitchen. At the end of each technique, you will put your new skill to the test by preparing a recipe that utilizes what you've learned. By the time you get to the end, you will have mastered all the basic cooking techniques. Trust me: You've got this.

PART TWO

Basic Techniques + Recipes

CHAPTER THREE

Measuring + Mixing

Cooking can be very creative, and though it's tempting to throw in a pinch of this and a bunch of that, it's still a good idea to learn the proper way to organize and measure your ingredients for best results. Once you've got the basics down, you can begin to improvise. In this chapter, we'll discuss the importance of having your ingredients organized and ready before you start cooking, how to accurately measure dry and wet ingredients, and the various methods of incorporating those ingredients to create your finished dish.

How to Organize Ingredients

Measuring all the ingredients you need to prepare a recipe beforehand is going to make cooking so much more enjoyable. This is what's known as *mise en place*, a French phrase meaning "everything in its place" (and even if you don't know French, it's still easy to pronounce—it sounds like "meez on plots").

Why is mise en place important? Well, rather than getting halfway through the recipe only to realize you don't have enough basil, you're going to assemble and measure everything beforehand. I know what you're thinking: "That's just going to add more time to my cooking!" But, in fact, it does just the opposite. When you have all your ingredients in front of you, cooking will take much less time and fewer mistakes will be made. Professional chefs and commercial kitchens do this prepping step every day. You don't think they're back there just waiting for your order before they dice every onion, do you? An example of mise en place can be found on most cooking shows—you have certainly seen those chefs with premeasured ingredients in little bowls, all set up to go when the camera rolls.

The other significant benefit to setting your mise en place is that it allows you to concentrate on your cooking. You won't have to race around the kitchen wondering if you already added the flour or whether it was the right amount. You'll be able to spend more time focusing on how your dish is coming along. Personally, I like to arrange my ingredients in the order they appear in the recipe on my counter, and add them as they are needed.

Measuring

A list of ingredients is great, but without knowing how much of each to put into a dish, it's not much help. That is where measurements come in. In a good recipe, each ingredient will include a unit of measure (1 cup, ½ teaspoon, etc.). But did you know there is a right way and a wrong way to measure ingredients? And a difference in how you measure dry and wet ingredients? Allow me to explain.

DRY INGREDIENTS

Dry ingredients refer to things such as flour, sugar, and baking soda. When cooking, these ingredients are measured using dry measuring cups. These are the metal or plastic nesting cups that typically come in sets containing 1-cup, ½-cup, ⅓-cup, and ¼-cup measures. To accurately measure dry ingredients, you either scoop or spoon the ingredient into the cup.

Remember not to pack it into the measuring cup (the exception to this rule is if the recipe calls for a "packed cup," like with brown sugar). Lastly, level it off with the back of a regular dinner knife so you get an accurate measurement. Use the back of the knife (the flat side) rather than the curved/sharp side so you get a nice, flat measurement.

The same technique is applied when measuring smaller amounts. But rather than using measuring cups, you use measuring spoons. Again, these are the metal or plastic nesting spoons that usually come in sets containing 1-tablespoon, 1-teaspoon, ½-teaspoon, and ¼-teaspoon measures. Scoop out the dry ingredient with the measuring spoon, and level it off with the back of a dinner knife.

WET INGREDIENTS

Wet ingredients refer to liquids, such as water, olive oil, and lemon juice. These should be measured in liquid measuring cups—often glass or plastic cups with measurements marked on the sides. They are typically sold in sets that include 1-cup, 2-cup, and 4-cup measures. Buy the entire set. You will use each size for various recipes. My favorite wet measuring cups are the ones you can read from above rather than having to lean over to the side. You'll get a more accurate reading that way.

While it may seem unnecessary to have two different types of measuring cups (one for wet and another for dry ingredients), there really is a difference. One cup of a liquid and one cup of a solid do vary enough when measured that it can determine how your recipe turns out, particularly when baking.

Everyday Seasoning

This easy-to-assemble seasoning mix is great on everything—chicken, beef, veggies, and more. Make a batch and keep it in your pantry so you'll have it when you need it.

Makes ¼ cup | Prep time: 5 minutes

TOOLS

Measuring spoons

Small zip-top bag, or
  Mason jar and lid

INGREDIENTS

1 tablespoon **kosher salt**

2¼ teaspoons freshly
  ground **black pepper**

¾ teaspoon dried **thyme**

¾ teaspoon **garlic powder**

Pinch ground
  cayenne pepper

1. In a small zip-top bag, combine the salt, black pepper, thyme, garlic powder, and cayenne. Seal the bag and shake well to distribute the spices.

2. Label the bag "Everyday Seasoning Mix" and store at room temperature.

➤ **Make It Easier:** This seasoning mixture will last for almost a year if kept in a cool, dark spot in your kitchen. Store it in a cabinet close to the stove but away from its direct heat.

Mixing

Mixing ingredients together sounds easy enough—and it is. But when it comes to cooking, there are a number of ways it can be done. Let's break it down.

STIR

Stirring is using a spoon or rubber spatula to mix and combine ingredients. Think of how you stir cream and sugar into your coffee. Stirring implies that you continue until all the ingredients are fully dissolved.

FOLD

Folding is a way to incorporate a delicate ingredient, such as whipped egg whites, into a dish that you want to keep intact. This is done using a rubber spatula. Start at the outside inner edge of the bowl, then turning the spatula toward the middle of the bowl, lifting the ingredients as you do. With whipped egg whites or cream, the intention is to maintain the airy quality of those ingredients so they don't deflate.

WHISK

You typically whisk food with a whisk (a wire metal kitchen hand tool) when you want to quickly break up ingredients to blend them. An example is preparing a vinaigrette, where you want the oil and vinegar to blend and stay together. Whisk quickly to emulsify (combine) the two ingredients.

Whisking is also used to incorporate air into an ingredient, such as eggs or cream. You must whisk quickly to make whipped cream or egg whites nice and fluffy.

TOSS

Tossing food can be done in two basic ways: in a pan over heat or in a bowl. In a pan, you can use tongs to toss the food, or shake the pan back and forth to move the food around; in a bowl, you can use tongs or two spoons to gently toss or move the food around to coat it with a dressing or sauce or evenly distribute the ingredients.

Honey-Citrus Vinaigrette

Impress your friends and family with this fresh, light vinaigrette that's just as delicious as it is easy to make. You'll find it especially tasty served over the Strawberry, Goat Cheese, and Arugula Salad (page 41).

Makes 1 cup | Prep time: 10 minutes

TOOLS

Liquid measuring cups
Measuring spoons
Whisk

INGREDIENTS

½ cup freshly squeezed **lemon juice**, lime juice, or orange juice

½ cup **extra-virgin olive oil**

2 teaspoons **honey**

Pinch **kosher salt**, plus more as needed

Pinch freshly ground **black pepper**, plus more as needed

Pinch ground **cayenne pepper**, plus more as needed (optional)

1. In a large liquid measuring cup, combine the lemon juice, olive oil, honey, salt, black pepper, and cayenne (if using). Use a whisk to quickly blend the ingredients.

2. Taste the dressing and add more salt, black pepper, and cayenne, as desired.

➤ **Beyond the Basics:** Recipes are just guidelines to follow. If you like a slightly sweeter dressing, add more honey. If you prefer it a bit spicier, throw in a pinch more cayenne. I like to double this recipe and store it in a Mason jar in the fridge. That way, you're not making a new batch every time you want a salad. Just give it a shake before each use.

CHAPTER FOUR

Knife Skills

Being able to use a knife confidently is, perhaps, the most critical skill to master in the kitchen. Once you've got that down, everything else comes easily. In this chapter, we'll cover everything from how to hold a knife properly to basic cuts. We'll have you chopping like a chef in no time!

How to Hold a Knife

Hold the knife handle in your dominant hand like you're shaking hands with it. Not a death grip—just a nice, easy, comfortable handshake. It's important to grip the handle so you have the greatest control of the knife. Your thumb should touch the inside top of the blade, just beyond the handle. Your pointer finger should be on the other side of the blade. Don't make the mistake of placing your index finger straight out on top of the knife—believe it or not, you'll have less control when you cut in that position. Your remaining three fingers should be curled around the bottom of the handle. This is the basic grip you will use with all knives.

Your other hand serves as your guiding hand, or the one that holds the food in place as you cut it. Keep your fingers curled up in a clawlike position, holding the food with your thumb and pinky finger, so that they are safely out of the way of the knife's blade. When you get really comfortable with the knife, you can use the knuckles of your curled-up hand as a guide to create consistently sized cuts.

Now, let's cover some of the basic cuts you'll use when cooking.

TRIM

Trimming means to clean a particular ingredient of excess material. Think of the fat on a chicken breast or a particularly fatty cut of beef. Typically, you'd cut these fatty parts off, right? And when it comes to fruits and vegetables, you might trim away long stalks from a head of broccoli or the woody ends of asparagus spears. Trimming here simply means cutting the ingredients neater so they're easier to eat.

SLICE

When you slice an ingredient, you cut uniform, flat pieces vertically with your knife. What you are slicing will determine which knife you choose. For small items, such as strawberries, a paring knife works well. For larger items, such as a steak or potato, choose a chef's knife. Ingredients such as tomatoes are best sliced with a serrated knife because it won't tear or squish them; the knife will easily slice right through.

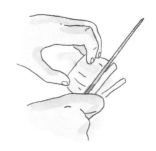

Curl the fingers of your guiding hand, hold the tomato with your thumb and pinky, and carefully slice the tomato from the top down until you cut through it. Repeat with equal-width slices until you reach the end of the tomato or you don't feel comfortable going any closer to your hand.

ROUGH CHOP

Rough chopping means to cut ingredients, usually with your chef's knife, and they don't all need to be the same size. This is the easiest of all the cuts. A good example of a rough chop would be when you cut up lettuce. To do this, simply place the tip of your knife on the cutting board and the heel of your guide hand on top of the blade. Move the knife back and forth while keeping the tip anchored, cutting the ingredient as you go.

DICE

Diced foods are cut smaller than chopped foods. They can vary in size from small to medium to large dice, but generally, you want to dice food into ¼-inch cubes. In this case, as opposed to a rough chop, you are aiming for a uniform size in your finished ingredient. This is important for two main reasons: Consistently sized food is more attractive in the finished dish, and it cooks more evenly than oddly sized pieces. For example, if you throw a ½-inch piece of carrot and a ¼-inch piece of carrot into a hot pan with oil at the same time and cook them for a few minutes, the larger piece will still be partly raw or a bit hard, whereas the smaller cut will be perfectly cooked or mushy.

Let's continue to use a carrot as an example of how to dice.

1 Holding the knife in your cutting, or dominant, hand and your guiding hand in a claw position, begin by cutting the carrot in half lengthwise.

2 Place the flat side of each carrot half on the cutting board so it won't slip.

3 Make as many lengthwise cuts as needed to cut planks that are ¼ inch thick.

4 Lay the long carrot planks flat on the cutting board, and cut lengthwise again so each strip is ¼ inch wide. At this point you should have long thin strips of carrots.

5 Line up the strips and, using your chef's knife, cut crosswise at ¼-inch intervals. You will end up with ¼-inch diced carrot pieces. Voilà!

MINCE

Minced food is even smaller than diced food. Keep in mind, you are still striving for uniform sizes and shapes. Garlic is one ingredient you often see minced in a recipe. To mince it, begin by dicing it. Finish by rocking your chef's knife back and forth across the small pile of diced garlic, just as you did with the rough chop, until the garlic pieces are very small in size. Minced food will cook very quickly because of its size, so be careful not to burn it.

OTHER CUTS

GRATE

Grating is typically done on a box grater—a four-sided, freestanding metal tool. Each side of the box grater has different sizes of holes, all for different purposes. Basically, grated foods come from the side with the smallest holes. The end result is food that looks almost powdered because it is shredded so small. Hard cheeses, such as Parmesan, are the ingredients you most often see grated in a recipe using this tool. Because grated foods are so small, they melt into the dish very quickly and thoroughly.

SHRED

Shredded foods are also prepped on a box grater, but you use the largest holes instead. They produce long, smooth strips of food. You will often see ingredients such as carrots and potatoes shredded using this tool. Shredded foods maintain some of their texture, but they also mix well with other ingredients in a dish.

ZEST

Zest is a term that usually refers to citrus, and it means to take off the outer colorful peel of the fruit; it can also refer to the peel itself. You zest because there is so much flavor in the peel—it's where all the natural oils in the fruit reside.

Citrus can be zested in a variety of ways. You can peel it with a paring knife, or use a handheld rasp (my favorite method) or even a box grater. Just be sure to use the smaller holes on the box grater. There are even specialty tools for removing zest.

Whichever method you use, be careful not to go too deep into the peel. When you start getting into the white part of the fruit (also known as the pith), just below the zest, it becomes really bitter, and that is not a particularly pleasant flavor. Stick close to the surface when zesting. In addition to bringing an amazingly fresh flavor to a dish, it can also serve as a colorful garnish.

PEEL

You peel foods when you want to remove an outer skin or rind that's tough, inedible, or unattractive. For example, you typically peel fruits such as oranges because the outer skin is inedible (although you definitely can use the zest). In other cases, you peel foods not because the skin is inedible but for textural reasons. For instance, you can definitely eat a potato's skin, but in certain recipes (extra-creamy mashed potatoes, page 124), you remove it to achieve the desired consistency.

The easiest way to peel most foods is with a vegetable peeler. There are some wonderful options on the market now that make peeling so much easier than the old-fashioned straight peeler. Look for *Y*-shaped, or even round, peelers. If you don't have a peeler, use a paring knife. Just be especially careful not to cut yourself.

CORE

To core a fruit or vegetable means to remove the center portion, or its core. You do this because it is hard and inedible. Examples of ingredients you would typically core for a recipe include apples, pineapples, and bell peppers. While there are specialty tools to remove cores, such as apple and pineapple corers, all you really need is your knife.

My favorite method for removing the core in apples, pears, and pineapples is to cut them into quarters and then, with one of the quarters sitting as flat against the cutting board as you can get it, place your knife at a 45-degree angle to the fruit, and cut the core straight down and out. Coring a bell pepper (also referred to as "seeding") is even easier. It can be done with just your hands by pulling out the seeds and the ribs.

Strawberry, Goat Cheese, and Arugula Salad

This is one of my all-time favorite recipes. It's so fresh and light. When strawberries are in season, there's nothing better. It comes together very quickly and easily. And if you have your salad dressing already made, it's even faster getting dinner on the table.

Serves 4 | Prep time: 15 minutes

TOOLS

Bowl, large
Cutting board
Dry measuring cups
Liquid measuring cup
Paring knife
Tongs

INGREDIENTS

6 cups **arugula**, washed and thoroughly dried

½ cup **Honey-Citrus Vinaigrette** (page 31, using orange juice)

1 cup **strawberries**, washed, thoroughly dried, tops removed and discarded, and sliced

¼ cup sliced toasted **almonds**

¼ cup **goat cheese**, crumbled

1. Place the arugula in a large bowl.

2. Add about half the dressing to the bowl. Using tongs, lightly toss the arugula with the salad dressing, making sure all the arugula is coated.

3. Divide the arugula between 4 appetizer plates.

4. Top each evenly with some strawberries, almonds, and goat cheese.

5. Drizzle the remaining dressing on top of the finished salad.

➤ **Swap It:** This recipe is fabulous as is, but you can change it up with the seasons. If you prefer peaches in summer or apples or pears in fall, substitute those for the strawberries. The same is true with the cheese. While the goat cheese is delicious, if you prefer Parmesan or Cheddar cheese, feel free to make that switch. And if you want to add a little protein to this salad, go ahead and throw some leftover grilled chicken or shrimp on top.

CHAPTER FIVE

Boiling

Boiling is a very basic method of cooking, whereby you submerge food in water and bring it to a very high temperature until it is cooked through. There are a number of ways it can be done—from gentle to rolling—and each has its own application, depending on what you're cooking. So, allow me to boil it all down for you.

How to Boil Water

We've all heard the old joke about the person who can't even boil water. If you've ever felt that way, fear not. I'll walk you through it in just three easy steps. Essentially, boiling water is heating it as quickly as you can until it gets to 212°F, at which point it bubbles rapidly.

Begin by placing a saucepan or pot full of water on the stovetop. I like to start with hot tap water in the pan. Cover the pot with a lid to help trap the heat. This will get the water to a boil faster.

Turn the burner to high and wait until large bubbles begin to rise to the surface. At that point, remove the lid so the water doesn't boil over. Congratulations! You've just boiled water.

Gentle Boil or Simmer

Now that you know the basics, let's talk specifics. Not all boils are the same. Some are more intense than others. With a gentle boil (sometimes referred to as a simmer), the bubbles barely break the surface of the water. A gentle boil is perfect when making poached eggs or cooking fresh ravioli. A more vigorous boil would cause the eggs to overcook and the ravioli to break apart. If you find your water starts to bubble too much, simply turn down the heat on the burner until the bubbles' movements slow.

Hardboiled Eggs

Hardboiled eggs are a great, portable source of protein, and are super easy to make. It's all about the timing. Follow the simple steps here and you'll have perfect hardboiled eggs every time.

Makes 12 eggs | Prep time: 5 minutes | Cook time: 15 minutes

TOOLS

Bowl, large

Medium saucepan
   (or larger as needed)
   with lid

Slotted spoon

INGREDIENTS

12 large **eggs**

1. Gently place the eggs in a saucepan large enough to hold them in a single layer.

2. Pour in enough cold water to cover the eggs by 1 inch.

3. Place the pan over high heat and bring the water to a boil.

4. Immediately turn off the heat, cover the pan, and let the eggs sit in the hot water for 11 minutes.

5. While the eggs cook, fill a bowl large enough to hold all the eggs with ice water. Set aside.

6. Using a slotted spoon, gently remove the eggs from the hot water and place them in the ice water to stop the cooking and to cool.

7. Drain the water and either peel the eggs to eat immediately or refrigerate them unpeeled for up to 1 week.

➢ **Beyond the Basics:** Gently crack the cooked egg on your kitchen counter and roll it around in your hands before peeling it under running water or in a bowl of water. The shell will come off more easily and you'll have less chance of tearing the egg as you peel it.

Rolling Boil

A rolling boil is a very vigorous boil in which large bubbles continuously make their way to the surface and are not slowed by stirring the pot. This is the method you will use to cook dried pasta, potatoes, and dense vegetables, such as carrots. To bring a pot of water to a rolling boil, follow the directions for how to boil water (see page 43).

Cacio e Pepe

This traditional Cacio e Pepe recipe takes just minutes to make and requires only seven ingredients. The phrase literally means "cheese and pepper." How simple is that? But it's so elegant in its simplicity that it makes the perfect impromptu recipe for pasta night. Pair it with a fresh salad, a crusty baguette, and a bottle of your favorite wine. Dinner is served!

Serves 6 | Prep time: 15 minutes | Cook time: 15 minutes

TOOLS

Box grater
Ladle
Large sauté pan or skillet
Large stockpot with lid
Tongs
Whisk

INGREDIENTS

3 tablespoons **kosher salt**, plus more as needed

1 pound **linguine** or spaghetti

4 tablespoons **butter**, divided

2 tablespoons **extra-virgin olive oil**

1 tablespoon freshly ground **black pepper**, large grind, plus more as needed

1½ cups freshly grated **Pecorino Romano cheese**, plus more for garnish

1½ cups freshly grated **Parmesan cheese**, plus more for garnish

1. Fill a large stockpot two-thirds full with water. Add the salt and stir to dissolve. Place the pot over high heat, cover it, and bring the water to a boil.

2. Add the linguine to the boiling water, stirring immediately so it doesn't stick to the pot and itself. Cook the pasta for 9 to 11 minutes (depending on the pasta you use), uncovered, until al dente (see page 13).

3. While the pasta cooks, melt 2 tablespoons of butter with the olive oil in a large sauté pan or skillet over medium heat. Add the pepper to the pan and cook until it is fragrant, about 1 minute.

4. Using a ladle, pour 1 cup of the pasta cooking water into the pan. Use a whisk to incorporate.

5. Once the pasta is cooked, using tongs, transfer the pasta from the pot of hot water to the sauté pan. Toss well to coat the pasta with the sauce.

6. Add the remaining 2 tablespoons of butter, continuing to toss the pasta thoroughly.

CONTINUED

7. Add the Pecorino Romano and Parmesan cheeses, and toss the pasta continuously until the cheese begins to melt. Remove the pan from the heat when you see that about half the cheese has melted.

8. If the sauce is too thick, add more pasta water to loosen the mixture.

9. Taste and season with salt and pepper to your liking. Remember, you can always add more, but it's hard to take it away if you add too much. Garnish the finished dish with extra cheese, if you like.

Steam

When water is converted to its vapor state at the boiling point—in other words, when water boils—the result is steam. Known as a moist-heat cooking method, steaming is one of the gentlest ways to cook something, because the food does not get agitated by bubbling liquid during the process.

Steaming has a number of benefits. Food stays moist as it is bathed in water vapor; the process also preserves more nutrients than other moist-heat cooking methods, as water-soluble nutrients (namely, vitamins B and C) aren't lost during cooking.

Because steaming is so gentle, it is perfect for cooking delicate foods. Along with popular dishes like Chinese dumplings, most vegetables and fish are ideal for steaming.

Although there are a lot of steamers available, made of everything from bamboo to plastic, steaming really doesn't require specialized equipment. For larger foods, such as pieces of meat or fish, you can improvise a steamer by placing a roasting rack in the bottom of a large pot and covering with a lid. Provided the cooking liquid you are using does not touch the food, you'll be steaming in no time.

For smaller foods, such as cut vegetables that would fall through a roasting rack, use an inexpensive steamer insert in a pot. You've probably seen these in various shops, markets, and even hardware stores. The diameter adjusts to fit whatever pot you put it in. If you don't have one, simply place a metal colander inside a large pot.

Steamed Broccoli Parmesan

Steaming is a great way to cook food quickly while retaining its valuable nutrients. This recipe is an elegant way to elevate a plain old vegetable to something special any night of the week. Enjoy it as a snack or a side to a main dish, such as fish, chicken, or tofu.

Serves 4 | Prep time: 10 minutes | Cook time: 10 minutes

TOOLS

Box grater
Chef's knife
Collapsible metal
    steamer insert
Cutting board
Large saucepan or pot
    with lid
Oven mitts
Tongs

INGREDIENTS

1 head **broccoli**,
    roughly chopped into
    bite-size pieces
4 tablespoons **butter**
¼ cup grated **Parmesan
    cheese**, plus more
    for garnish
Kosher salt
Freshly ground
    black pepper

1. Fill a large saucepan or pot with water until it reaches a depth of 1 inch. Place a steamer insert into the pan. Make sure the water is not higher than the holes in the steamer insert. If you have too much water and can see it coming through the insert, pour some out. Place the pan over high heat, cover it, and bring the water to a boil.

2. Once the water begins to steam, place the broccoli in the steamer insert in the pan. Cover and let steam for 5 minutes, or until the broccoli is bright green and tender but not mushy. Using oven mitts, carefully remove the broccoli and steamer insert from the pot and drain the water.

3. Return the broccoli to the pot, add the butter and Parmesan cheese, and season with salt and pepper. Using tongs, gently toss the broccoli, mixing well until the butter melts and the broccoli is coated in the mixture.

4. Serve the broccoli with a little more Parmesan cheese sprinkled on top.

CHAPTER SIX

Pan Cooking

When you're cooking on the stovetop, it's just you and the food. This is not like baking, where you can sit back, set the timer, and wait. Whether you are sautéing or searing, frying or stir-frying, you are actively participating—constantly watching and adjusting, making sure the food is hot enough but not too hot, fully cooked but not overcooked. This is full-contact cooking.

How to Harness Heat

It's been said that cooking isn't really cooking until you introduce a little heat. To do that, you need to start with a good-quality pan. Be sure to get the pan hot before you put anything in it. A good way to test if it's ready is to hold your hand over the pan. If you can easily feel the heat and still hold your hand there for a few seconds, it's hot enough. At that point, add your fat. If you're using butter, let it melt completely, swirling the pan so the fat covers the entire surface. Now you're ready to add your food. No sizzle? The pan isn't hot enough. This means whatever you add to the pan will absorb the fat, making it greasy rather than crispy.

Sauté

The French term *sauté* literally means "to jump," in reference to the food moving around in the pan. It is a method of cooking that uses high heat for a short period of time—and it's a great way to get dinner on the table in a hurry. When you sauté, choose a wide, shallow pan in which you can toss or stir ingredients frequently until they are cooked. Because you're cooking quickly, the ingredients need enough room so that the water they naturally release during cooking can evaporate. If water sits in the pan too long, the food will begin to steam instead of sauté, which means it will also have a different texture.

A little fat in the pan will also contribute flavor and keep things from sticking to the hot surface. More importantly, fat also helps deliver heat into ingredients when they're moved around in the pan with a wooden spoon, tongs, or a spatula, so they cook faster.

Speedy Shrimp Sauté

Shrimp is one of the all-time best ingredients to have on hand when you want something quick to cook. Eat it on its own or serve it over hot pasta, on top of rice, or with a side of toasted French bread.

Serves 4 | Prep time: 5 minutes | Cook time: 10 minutes

TOOLS

Bowl, medium
Liquid measuring cup
Measuring spoons
Paring knife
Sauté pan or skillet, preferably 10 inches or larger
Tongs
Wooden spoon

INGREDIENTS

2 tablespoons **butter**
1 pound **shrimp**, peeled and deveined (see Beyond the Basics tip)
2 **garlic cloves**, minced
¼ cup **dry white wine**
Juice of ½ **lemon**
2 tablespoons torn fresh **basil**
Kosher salt
Freshly ground **black pepper**

1. Place a large sauté pan or skillet over medium-high heat and add the butter to melt.

2. Add the shrimp to the hot pan and sauté for about 3 minutes, turning them with tongs, until they just turn pink.

3. Add the garlic to the pan and cook for 30 seconds, or until you can really smell the garlic, stirring constantly so it does not burn. Using tongs, gently transfer the shrimp from the pan into a bowl and set aside.

4. While the pan is still on medium-high heat, pour in the white wine. Deglaze the pan by scraping up any brown bits from the bottom of the pan with a wooden spoon (see page 85).

5. Return the shrimp to the pan. Pour the lemon juice over the shrimp, and toss to combine the shrimp with the sauce.

6. Garnish with the basil and season with salt and pepper.

➤ **Beyond the Basics:** If you haven't bought the shrimp already peeled and deveined, you can learn to do so yourself. To peel the shrimp, remove the tough outer shell and discard it. To devein the shrimp, using a paring knife, cut along the entire top length of the shrimp, about ¼ inch deep, and remove the dark vein. Rinse the shrimp before using.

Fry

Frying is similar to sautéing. But whereas sautéing uses very little oil, frying often requires a bit more. Much like sautéing, it's key to get the oil to a certain temperature before adding your food. The magic number is 350°F—anything less and your food will be greasy; anything much higher and it will burn before it cooks through. The best way to judge the temperature of the oil is using a candy thermometer.

Generally, when frying, use a vegetable or peanut oil, both of which have higher smoke points than olive oil. In other words, they will be able to withstand the higher temperatures of frying without burning.

Pan-Fried Bacon

As the old saying goes, everything is better with bacon . . . and I couldn't agree more!

Serves 4 | Prep time: 5 minutes | Cook time: 15 minutes

TOOLS

Paper towels

Plate

Sauté pan or skillet, preferably 10 inches or larger

Tongs

INGREDIENTS

1 pound **bacon**, preferably applewood smoked

1. Line a plate with paper towels and set aside.

2. Place the bacon slices in a single, even layer in a cold sauté pan or skillet.

3. Place the pan on the stovetop and turn the heat to medium-high. Cook the bacon for 4 to 7 minutes, until it is well browned on one side. As the bacon fat renders (melts) out, the bacon may pop and sizzle.

4. Using tongs, flip the bacon and cook the other side for 4 to 5 minutes more, until well browned.

5. Using tongs, transfer the cooked bacon to the prepared plate so the excess oil can drain. Pat the top with another paper towel to get rid of the grease.

> **Beyond the Basics:** Typically, when we talk about frying, it's vital to get your pan hot before adding the food. Bacon is an exception to that rule. To get those beautiful long strips of fried bacon, start it in a cold pan. If you use a hot pan, the bacon will curl up and won't be as long and lean.

Stir-Fry

Stir-frying originated in China. It's a method to cook food quickly in oil over very high heat—usually inside a wok. Sounds a lot like sautéing, right? It is very similar, indeed. The basic difference is that you crank the heat even higher when you stir-fry. And although woks are the traditional vessels for stir-frying, this technique can be done in any skillet or sauté pan. Just be sure to get the oil hot before you add the ingredients, and watch the heat. Turn it down if it seems too hot or the pan begins to smoke—and remember to stir, stir, stir. Why do you think they call it stir-frying?

Stir-Fried Green Beans

If you never liked eating your green beans as a child, chances are you never had them prepared like this. My Chinese takeout–inspired spin takes this occasionally boring veggie to a whole new level. To make a meal out if it, just throw some pre-cooked chicken or shrimp on top.

Serves 4 | Prep time: 10 minutes | Cook time: 15 minutes

TOOLS

Chef's knife

Cutting board

Liquid measuring cup

Measuring spoons

Sauté pan or skillet, preferably 10 inches or larger

Tongs

Whisk

INGREDIENTS

¼ cup **soy sauce**

¼ teaspoon **sesame oil**

½ teaspoon **red pepper flakes**

2 tablespoons **vegetable oil**

1 pound fresh **green beans**, washed and ends trimmed

2 **garlic cloves**, minced

1-inch piece fresh **ginger**, peeled and minced, or 1 teaspoon ground ginger

¼ cup sliced **almonds** (optional)

Kosher salt

Freshly ground **black pepper**

1. In a liquid measuring cup, use a whisk to whisk the soy sauce, sesame oil, and red pepper flakes until combined. Set aside.

2. Place a sauté pan or skillet over medium-high heat.

3. Add the vegetable oil and heat it until it shimmers and moves easily around the pan.

4. Add the green beans, cooking them in batches if your pan cannot hold all of them at once. Using tongs, move the green beans around the pan so each is coated with some oil. Cook for about 10 minutes, stirring constantly, until the green beans are tender but not overly cooked.

5. Just before you are ready to take the green beans out of the pan, add the garlic, ginger, and almonds (if using), and cook for 30 seconds more, or just until you can smell the garlic. Repeat with the remaining green beans, as needed.

6. If you've cooked the green beans in batches, return them all to the pan. Pour the sauce over the green beans and stir to coat them well. Taste and season with salt and pepper.

Sear

Searing is a technique that involves cooking food over very intense heat to create a brown crust on the exterior. It makes food more attractive and flavorful. Because you are working with very high temperatures, you need to use the proper oil. Olive oil is not a good choice because it has a low smoke point. Opt instead for oils such as vegetable or peanut. They can take intense heat for much longer without burning.

To get the best sear, it's very important to get your pan and the oil really hot before adding the food. If you don't, you won't get the beautiful brown crust you're going for.

Cast-Iron Rib Eye Steak

There are few things better than a properly cooked steak. And the good news is, you don't need a grill when you have a properly seasoned cast-iron skillet. Get at least 1-inch-thick steaks, preferably 1¼-inch-thick steaks, for the best flavor. Serve with a side of homemade, hand-cut Roasted Sweet Potato Fries (page 123), or enjoy them on their own.

Serves 2 | Prep time: 30 minutes | Cook time: 10 minutes

TOOLS

Aluminum foil

Cast-iron skillet or
   grill pan

Instant-read thermometer

Large spoon

Tongs

INGREDIENTS

2 (8-ounce) **rib eye steaks**,
   at room temperature

2 tablespoons
   **Montreal-style steak
   seasoning** or Everyday
   Seasoning (page 27)

3 tablespoons **butter**

1. Remove the steaks from the refrigerator at least 30 minutes before cooking them so they can come to room temperature.

2. Season both sides of the steaks with the Montreal-style seasoning.

3. Place the skillet over high heat.

4. Place the steaks in the hot pan and let them cook for about 3 minutes, undisturbed, until you begin to see a little brown on the bottom edges of the steaks.

5. Using tongs, flip the steaks. They should be deeply browned. If not, flip them back to their original side until they turn dark brown. At that point, cook the opposite side until deeply browned, about 3 minutes more.

6. Add the butter to the pan and let it melt. Using a large spoon, ladle the butter over the steaks, which helps flavor them.

CONTINUED

Cast-Iron Rib Eye Steak CONTINUED

7. Check your steaks for doneness. Until you get comfortable with how long it takes to cook a steak to your preferred doneness, use your instant-read thermometer and refer to the temperatures on page 17.

8. Remove the steaks from the skillet and lightly cover them with aluminum foil to keep warm. Let them rest for about 5 minutes. If you cut the steaks too soon, they will become tough and dry, losing all the delicious juices.

> **Beyond the Basics:** Eventually you'll be able to tell how done a steak is simply by touching it. You will use your palm as your guide. This method is called—naturally—the touch test.

> > **Rare:** With your palm facing up, touch your index finger to your thumb. With your other hand, push on the fleshy part at the base of your hand where your thumb is attached. That is what rare meat feels like.

> > **Medium-Rare:** Now touch your middle finger to your thumb and press down on the same spot. That is what medium-rare meat feels like.

> > **Medium-Well:** Placing your ring finger against your thumb, press down against the base of your thumb. That is what medium-well meat feels like. As you can tell, the more the meat is cooked, the firmer it becomes.

CHAPTER SEVEN

Oven Cooking

In this chapter, we're going to let the oven do all the cooking. From baking to broiling, it is the perfect way to surround your food with constant heat.

How to Let the Oven Do All the Work

First, it's a good idea to preheat your oven before you put the food in. Recipe cook times are based on a hot oven. If you put food into a cold oven, it will take longer to cook. Plus, your finished dish will be cooked much more unevenly, because it had to go through a series of temperatures from cold to hot. Keep in mind that it takes 10 to 15 minutes to preheat your oven, depending on how old it is and how hot you want it to be. You'll want to get into the habit of turning it on before you begin doing anything else so it's ready when you are.

Where you place the food in the oven is also very important. The ideal place to bake is in the center of the oven, which is where the air circulates the best. If you have multiple items to bake, stagger the dishes or trays so one doesn't cover another, or else it will prevent hot air from getting to all of the items.

If you're worried the food is not going to heat evenly, consider using the convection setting on your oven (if you have one). When you choose convection bake or roast, you engage the fan at the back of the oven. This means it moves the hot air much more quickly and efficiently around the inside of the oven. As a result, you will need to lower the oven temperature by 25 degrees and reduce the cooking time, as well. There is no hard-and-fast rule about how to adjust the cooking time. Just remember that you can always check your dish and continue cooking. But it is much more difficult to save a dish that is burnt.

If you prefer not to use the convection setting (or you don't have one), you can always rotate the trays or pans around in the oven. This is a particularly good idea if you find your oven bakes too hot in one area. For example, if every time you bake cookies, the ones in the back left corner burn, that's a good indication you need to rotate your pans during the cooking process.

Having said that, don't open the oven door frequently. Every time you do, you let precious hot air escape, which lowers the temperature in the oven. Keep in mind that you can use the oven light and peer through the window, if your oven is so equipped, instead of opening the door. This rule is most important to remember when making baked goods—especially bread, muffins, and cakes. Frequent disruptions to the cooking temperature will result in flat, dense cakes and bread.

Roast

Roasting food means surrounding it with dry heat from all sides. While roasting is usually done in the oven, it can also take place over an open outdoor fire. Foods can be roasted at low, medium, or high temperatures. Foods that are typically roasted are chicken, turkey, beef roasts, vegetables, and even marshmallows. The temperature you choose depends on the food you are cooking. Large cuts, such as a turkey or a rib roast, benefit from a lower temperature and longer cooking time, whereas vegetables are best roasted at a medium temperature. Smaller cuts, such as steaks, are best cooked at a higher temperature.

Having the right equipment is key to roasting. For recipes such as roasted turkey and beef roast, think about investing in a sturdy, metal, heavy-duty roasting pan with low sides and handles. It helps if it has a rack that fits inside the pan to keep the food off the bottom, allowing the juices to drip down while preventing the food from sitting in the moisture, which can make it soggy.

Finally, for larger cuts, it's really nice to have a thermometer to determine when the meat is properly cooked. Instant-read thermometers are fine, but for about $25, a digital probe thermometer is invaluable when it comes to cooking food to just the right temperature. You set the thermometer to the desired temperature, and it monitors while the food cooks. When the internal temperature of the meat reaches your desired temperature, the thermometer will sound an audible alarm, indicating it's time to remove the dish from the heat.

If you are cooking a large cut of meat, let it rest for 10 to 20 minutes after it comes out of the oven. Like the Cast-Iron Rib Eye Steak (page 61) from the previous chapter, if you cut into the meat too soon after taking it out of the oven, the juices will run out and the meat will become dry.

Rosemary-Roasted Root Vegetables

Roasting is an easy way to get amazing flavor out of your food that does not require a great deal of effort. The oven does all the hard work. Although root vegetables are at their peak in winter months, you can still find them year-round. This recipe would be a perfect complement to Maple-Roasted Pork Tenderloin with Apples (page 137) for a fabulous fall dinner.

Serves 4 | Prep time: 15 minutes | Cook time: 25 minutes

TOOLS

Bowl, large

Chef's knife

Cutting board

Large sheet pan

Measuring spoons

Metal fish spatula or tongs

Oven mitts

Vegetable peeler

INGREDIENTS

1 **butternut squash**, peeled and cut into 1½-inch chunks

2 **parsnips**, peeled and cut into chunks

2 **carrots**, peeled and cut into chunks

2 medium **onions**, quartered

1 teaspoon dry rosemary, or 1 tablespoon fresh **rosemary**

2 tablespoons **extra-virgin olive oil**

¾ teaspoon freshly ground **black pepper**, divided

¼ teaspoon **kosher salt**

1. Place a rimmed sheet pan in the oven and pre-heat the oven to 400°F.

2. In a large bowl, combine the squash, parsnips, carrots, onions, rosemary, olive oil, pepper, and salt. Toss to coat the veggies in the oil and spices. Place the vegetables on the hot sheet pan, spreading them in a single layer so they do not overlap.

3. Roast the vegetables for about 25 minutes, using a metal fish spatula or tongs to turn them half-way through, until they are tender and browned.

➤ Swap It: Parsnips look like white carrots but have an earthy, sweet flavor all their own, especially when roasted. If you can't find them or if you don't like them, try Brussels sprouts—another winter vegetable. If you use Brussels sprouts, they just need their root ends trimmed flat and any discolored leaves removed before adding them to the bowl. Although this recipe calls for root vegetables, it's just as great in the summer with zucchini, yellow squash, and mushrooms.

Bake

Baking means to cook food by surrounding it with dry heat, typically in an oven. Common types of foods that are baked include breads, cakes, and potatoes. Although baking still requires your attention, this method of cooking does have a certain "set it and forget it" quality. Rather than having to constantly stir or whisk, with baking, you can pop food in the oven, set a timer, and go about other tasks.

Banana Bread

If you want your house to smell amazing while using up those last few bananas that have seen better days, whip up a loaf of this tasty treat. It's great in the morning with a cup of coffee or as a pick-me-up snack in the afternoon. It's even better grilled with a scoop of vanilla ice cream and some caramel sauce on top.

Makes 1 loaf | Prep time: 15 minutes | Cook time: 1 hour

TOOLS

9-by-5-inch loaf pan
Bowls, 2 medium
Handheld electric mixer or
    stand mixer
Oven mitts
Rubber spatula
Toothpick

INGREDIENTS

Nonstick cooking spray

8 tablespoons (1 stick)
    butter, at room
    temperature

1 cup **sugar**

2 large **eggs**, whisked

3 ripe **bananas**

1 teaspoon **vanilla extract**

2 cups **all-purpose flour**

1 teaspoon **kosher salt**

1 teaspoon **baking soda**

¾ cup **walnuts**, chopped
    (optional)

1. Preheat the oven to 350°F. Coat a 9-by-5-inch loaf pan with cooking spray. Set aside.

2. In a medium bowl, using a handheld electric mixer, stand mixer, or spatula, beat the sugar and butter until they are light and fluffy.

3. Add the eggs and mix until they are thoroughly incorporated.

4. Add the bananas and vanilla, and mix until the bananas are softened and well incorporated into the mixture.

5. In another medium bowl, stir together the flour, salt, and baking soda. Add the flour mixture to the banana mixture and use a rubber spatula to stir just until moistened. Do not overmix or the bread will be tough. Fold in the walnuts (if using) and pour the batter into the prepared loaf pan.

6. Bake for about 1 hour, or until a toothpick inserted into the center comes out clean—in other words, with no batter adhering to it.

➤ **Make It Easier:** If you forgot to take the butter out to soften, fear not. You can grate it using the largest holes of a box grater and the butter will be perfect to use in this recipe.

Broil

Broiling is cooking food in the oven under intense heat. If you look inside your oven, you may see a heating element at the top. (Some ovens have a broiler in a bottom drawer, below the main oven, and some ovens have top and bottom broil options.) Broiling is a great way to cook food very quickly, brown it, and give it a crunch. Many people fail to take advantage of this easy method. Here's how you can.

Broilers typically have just two settings: on and off. It doesn't get much easier than that! But while it's a simple way to cook, broiling does require you to stay close by.

Location is everything when it comes to broiling, so move your rack as close to the broiling unit as possible. Preheat the broiler. It will come up to temperature much quicker than the Bake setting, usually in about 5 minutes.

It's a good idea to leave the oven door cracked a bit while you're broiling. It will get very hot in there very quickly, and you don't want flare-ups from any oil to ignite. It also allows any steam or smoke to escape.

Open-Face Tuna Melt

Tuna melts are one of life's guilty pleasures—not all that sophisticated but oh-so delicious. This diner classic is simply crunchy toasted bread topped with mounds of luscious tuna salad enrobed in gooey melted cheese. What's not to love?

Serves 2 | Prep time: 10 minutes | Cook time: 5 minutes

TOOLS

Bowl, medium

Box grater

Can opener

Chef's knife

Fork

Measuring spoons

Metal fish spatula

Oven mitts

Small sheet pan

INGREDIENTS

2 (3-ounce) cans **tuna** packed in water, drained well

1½ tablespoons **mayonnaise**

1 teaspoon **Dijon mustard**

¼ **onion**, finely diced

2 tablespoons **pickle relish** (optional)

Kosher salt

Freshly ground **black pepper**

2 slices **ciabatta bread**, toasted

1 cup shredded **Cheddar cheese**

1. Preheat the broiler and position an oven rack in the top position but not so close that the food will touch the heat source.

2. Place the tuna in a medium bowl and use a fork to break it up.

3. Add the mayonnaise, mustard, onion, and relish (if using), and season with salt and pepper. Stir to mix well.

4. Place the toast on a work surface and spread each with half the tuna mixture. Place the bread on a sheet pan.

5. Place the open-face sandwiches under the broiler for about 3 minutes to warm the tuna, keeping an eye on them to prevent burning.

6. Using a metal fish spatula, remove them from the broiler and top each sandwich with half of the Cheddar cheese. Return the sandwiches to the broiler for 2 minutes, or until the cheese melts but before it burns.

➤ **Swap It:** I recommend a crusty artisan-style loaf to make these melts, but any hearty bread will do. You definitely want a bread with some texture to hold the tuna. Toasted English muffins are great here, too. Also, feel free to swap the Cheddar cheese for any other easy-melting cheese, like pepper Jack or Swiss.

CHAPTER EIGHT

Building Flavor

Congratulations on making it to the last tutorial chapter! You've mastered the basics, and now it's time to take everything you've learned to the next level. In this chapter, we're bumping up the flavor in a big way.

How to Add More Flavor

Our taste buds recognize four basic flavors: salty, sweet, sour, and bitter. A fifth has recently been added to the list: umami, a savory, meaty flavor. The best dishes bring some or all of these elements into play to awaken the palate. When you're creating a dish, you should strive to balance these flavors. Too much of any one is boring and often overwhelming. Think of a super-sweet dessert. The first bite might be great, but it quickly becomes too sweet. Now think of the same dessert with salted caramel on top and maybe a bit of diced jalapeño sprinkled on it. The interplay of sweet with salty and even a bit of spice makes it much more interesting. Let's take a minute to explore in depth each of the ways you can build more complex flavors in a dish.

Salt

Salt is a natural flavor enhancer. Added judiciously, it awakens the flavors of food like no other ingredient. If you don't believe me, buy a bag of unsalted potato chips and a bag of salted ones and do a taste test. Which do you like better?

Basically, there are three types of salt: table, kosher, and sea salt. *For all recipes in this book, assume you are using kosher salt, unless otherwise specified.*

Table salt is the stuff many of us grew up on. Its crystals are very uniform in size (small), and it often has iodine added. If you have a sensitive palate, you might notice a slightly bitter or metallic taste due to the iodine. It is partly for this reason that many professional cooks don't like to use table salt. Instead, most prefer to cook with kosher salt.

Kosher salt, which is made by applying pressure to salt during the manufacturing process (usually with rollers), is larger grained and less dense than table salt. This is important because, if you're measuring by the teaspoon, you'll get less of a salty taste than you would with the same amount of table salt. Also, although it is called "kosher," it doesn't refer to the salt itself being kosher—almost every salt is kosher! It's because kosher salt, with its large crystalline structure, is used to remove the moisture and blood from meats. This process, similar to dry brining, is called koshering, and is one of the processes that makes kosher meat kosher.

Sea salt, the last basic type of salt, is typically a by-product of solar evaporation—letting salty water from the sea or salt lakes evaporate in shallow pools through exposure to sun and wind, then gathering the resulting salt. Consequently, this is a much more expensive process, which makes sea salts pricier than their table and kosher counterparts.

Sea salts are typically considered "finishing salts," meaning they are often used at the end of a dish. Whereas you would sauté or bake with kosher salt, you would save sea salts for the final presentation, taking advantage of their best assets—color and texture. Common types of sea salts include fleur de sel, sel gris, Hawaiian lava salt (it's black!), and Maldon sea salt (with crystals shaped like little pyramids). Himalayan salt, although not from the sea, is prized for its gorgeous pink color and can range from finely ground to very coarse in texture. It's beautiful sprinkled on top of dark chocolates. Finishing salts are all fun to experiment with. Give them a try.

Heat

When we talk about heat in this section, we're referring to how spicy an ingredient is. This category includes things such as black pepper, cayenne, red pepper flakes, and a whole array of fresh hot peppers. There are literally thousands of hot peppers to choose from, each with its own degree of intensity.

Heat is not as vital to a dish as salt is, but it sure livens up the party. Usually you'll feel it on the back end, or just as you are finishing the bite. Unless you like food really spicy, most people prefer moderate heat. So, know your guests and add it sparingly. You can always offer additional heat at the table for those who want it. Here are some forms of extra heat:

Sriracha, a hot sauce made from chile peppers, distilled vinegar, garlic, salt, and sugar.

Tabasco or other hot sauces, made from tabasco or other red chile peppers, distilled vinegar, and salt.

Harissa, a paste typically made from various dried red chile peppers, cumin, coriander, caraway seeds, and garlic.

Wasabi, which is made from wasabi root. Be careful with it (a little goes a long way).

Horseradish, a spicy root that is grated to add zip to dishes, and is available in prepared forms, as well. Similar to wasabi, it is very potent!

Fats

Fats are vital to cooking. Whereas salt enhances flavors, fat brings its own. Just imagine a BLT without bacon or mayonnaise, fried chicken without oil, or macaroni without cheese. It's just not the same. From olive oil and butter to eggs and cheeses. They deliver a richness and full-bodied flavor to dishes unlike any other ingredient and help distribute the flavors already present in the dish over the palate because of their silky texture.

Fat is also a very versatile addition to the pantry as it plays three distinct roles in the kitchen:

· It can be added as an ingredient, such as bacon to a BLT.

· It can be used as the cooking medium (French fries cooked in oil).

· It can be used as a seasoning, such as when you finish a sauce with a swirl of butter or drizzle a bit of olive oil over roasted vegetables just before serving.

A world without fats is a world without flavor.

Acid

An acid is anything that tastes sour. Good sources of acid in the kitchen include vinegar, citrus juice, wine, beer, pickles, and tomatoes, to name just a few. You may be asking, "What's the big deal about using acids in cooking?" Think of it this way: You use salt to *enhance* flavor, and you add acids to *balance* flavors. During cooking, you might use wine or stock to deglaze the pan (as we will when we make Chicken Gravy, page 86) or tomatoes in Guacamole (page 115). Each of those acids helps balance the flavors of the other ingredients in the dish.

After cooking, you add an acid when you want to improve the flavor of the dish and balance it out. For example, Fresh Fish

Tacos (page 151) are great on their own, but if you add a squirt of fresh lime juice just before serving, they will be even better. Common acidic ingredients with which to finish a dish include lemon juice, lime juice, balsamic vinegar, feta cheese, and olives (as with Greek Salad, page 121). Adding acids to a dish is the next step in your cooking journey. It takes a bit of finesse to master, but it is worth the effort.

Herbs + Aromatics

Herbs are the fragrant leaves and tender stems of green plants that give a dish a delicate, almost floral, flavor. Common examples include basil, cilantro, dill, oregano, parsley, and thyme. Available fresh or dried, some of both is nice to have on hand. Just know that although they are not entirely interchangeable, the general rule of thumb is to substitute 1 teaspoon of dried herbs for 1 tablespoon of fresh herbs, and vice versa. But let taste be your guide.

Having said that, there really is no comparison in a dish between using fresh or dried herbs. Each has its respective job. Dried herbs are best used early in a recipe so they have time to rehydrate and allow their oils to infuse the dish with flavor. Fresh herbs are best added right before serving the dish. If allowed to cook too long, their vibrant color and flavor dissipate.

Some herbs naturally go well with others. Here are some classic herb and spice combinations for you to try.

Bouquet garni: basil, bay leaf, oregano, parsley

Pungent: black pepper, celery, chile peppers, cumin, curry, ginger

Herbal: basil, marjoram, rosemary, thyme

Spicy: black pepper, cinnamon, ginger, star anise

Hot: chile peppers, cilantro, cumin, garlic

Sweet: allspice, anise, cinnamon, cloves, nutmeg

➤ **Word to the wise:** When you double a recipe that uses bold herbs and spices (like garlic, cayenne, and curry), use only 1½ times the original amount. Otherwise, the taste might be too strong.

Another great way to build flavor is with aromatics. This is just a fancy term for a combination of ingredients that you heat in fat to unlock their flavors. I'm betting you've already done this and didn't even know it. A classic blend of aromatics is what the French call *mirepoix*, a combination of onion, carrot, and celery cooked down in a bit of fat before starting a soup. In Cajun and Creole cuisine, it's known as the Holy Trinity and consists of onion, celery, and bell pepper. *Sofrito* is the version common to Spanish cuisine and usually consists of onion, garlic, and peppers or tomatoes, though ingredients vary by region.

Regardless of what you start with, heating aromatics in fat releases their flavors, thereby deepening the intensity of the dish. Sauces, stocks, soups, stews, and curries all depend on aromatics to build flavor.

Roasted Chicken

Now it's time to take what you just learned and practice on a bird. With a combination of salt, heat, acid, herbs, and fats, you can roast a succulent chicken that will make your mouth water.

Serves 4 | Prep time: 20 minutes | Cook time: 1 hour 15 minutes

TOOLS

Aluminum foil

Chef's knife

Cutting board

Instant-read thermometer

Kitchen twine

Liquid measuring cup

Measuring spoons

Metal roasting pan
    with rack

Oven mitts

Paper towels

Spoon

Vegetable peeler

INGREDIENTS

1 whole (4- to 5-pound)
    roasting chicken

2 **carrots,**
    roughly chopped

2 **celery stalks,**
    roughly chopped

1 **onion**, roughly chopped

1 **lemon**, halved

2 **rosemary sprigs**

4 tablespoons
    butter, melted

2 tablespoons **Everyday
    Seasoning** (page 27)

4 **garlic cloves,** minced

1. Preheat the oven to 450°F.

2. Remove and discard the bag of giblets from inside the chicken.

3. Place the carrots, celery, and onion in the bottom of a roasting pan. Position the rack over the vegetables.

4. Place the lemon halves and rosemary sprigs inside the chicken's cavity.

5. Truss the chicken with kitchen twine by tying the legs together. Tuck the wings underneath the bird's body. Set aside.

6. In a liquid measuring cup, stir together the melted butter, Everyday Seasoning, and garlic until well incorporated.

7. Gently lift the skin of the chicken at the neck, just enough to be able to spread butter underneath it. Using your hands and starting at the breasts, pour the melted butter mixture under the skin, rubbing it all over to coat. Rub whatever is left on the outside of the skin. Nestle the chicken, breast-side up, onto the roasting rack.

8. Roast for 15 minutes.

CONTINUED

Roasted Chicken CONTINUED

9. Reduce the oven's temperature to 350°F and continue to roast for 1 hour, or until the chicken reaches an internal temperature of 165°F, measured with an instant-read thermometer or meat thermometer. The juices should run clear when you cut into it.

10. Remove the chicken from the oven and cover it lightly with aluminum foil. Let rest for 20 to 30 minutes.

11. Remove the carrots, celery, and onion from the roasting pan. Cut and remove the trussing strings from the chicken before slicing and serving.

12. Optional: Set aside the roasting pan to make Chicken Gravy (page 86).

To properly carve your bird for serving

1. Place the bird, breast-side up, on a cutting board.

2. Using a sharp knife, cut between the breast and each leg, cutting all the way through. Remove the leg and thigh from the bird.

3. Using your hand, pull the wings from the bird.

4. With your knife, slice the breast meat off the bone.

➤ **Beyond the Basics:** To get the most flavor and juiciness from your bird, flip it! That's right. About halfway through the roasting time, turn the bird over completely to redistribute the juices. Just before taking it out of the oven, turn it breast-side up. It will be perfectly roasted and delicious.

Deglaze

Deglazing means to pour liquid into a hot pan that's just been used to cook fish, meats, poultry, or vegetables to loosen and remove the stuck-on browned bits (or drippings). Those brown bits are packed with tasty umami flavor you can incorporate into a sauce or gravy. To deglaze, place your pan over medium-high heat, gently pour in about ¼ cup of liquid (such as wine, stock, or water), and whisk as you pour, scraping the bottom of the pan to remove the bits. That's all there is to it. Not only is it a great way to get a head start on cleaning your pan, but it releases amazing flavor that would otherwise go down the drain.

Chicken Gravy

Roasted chicken is delicious all on its own, but it's over-the-top good with gravy. If you're a little intimated by the idea of making gravy, fear not. This recipe is foolproof. Of course, you'll need to start with that roasting pan that just came out of the oven with the Roasted Chicken (page 83) and its drippings.

Serves 4 | Prep time: 10 minutes | Cook time: 10 minutes

TOOLS
Dry measuring cup
Liquid measuring cup
Whisk

INGREDIENTS
Chicken drippings from Roasted Chicken (page 83)
¼ cup **all-purpose flour**
2 cups **chicken broth**
Kosher salt
Freshly ground **black pepper**
Pinch **cayenne pepper**

1. Pour out all but 4 tablespoons of the chicken drippings from the pan.

2. Place the roasting pan over medium-high heat and, using a whisk, incorporate the flour so it forms a paste with the remaining chicken drippings. Cook, whisking constantly, for 2 minutes. The mixture will begin to turn brown. Be careful not to burn it, turning the heat down, if needed.

3. While whisking continuously, slowly pour in the chicken broth and whisk until the gravy is smooth. Cook, whisking, until the gravy comes to a boil and thickens.

4. Taste and season the gravy with salt, black pepper, and a pinch of cayenne.

PART THREE

Recipes That Bring It All Together

Breakfast

Creamy Blueberry Banana Smoothie

Smoothies are the perfect breakfast—everything you need in one glass. If you're in a hurry, you can't beat a smoothie to get your day started.

Serves 2 | Prep time: 10 minutes

TOOLS

Blender

Dry measuring cups

Liquid measuring cup

Measuring spoons

Paring knife

INGREDIENTS

1 ripe **banana**, cut into 2-inch pieces

½ cup fresh **blueberries**

1 cup **yogurt** (plain, vanilla, or flavored)

¼ cup **milk** or juice of choice, plus more as needed

1 tablespoon **honey**

1½ cups **ice**, plus more as needed

1. In a blender, combine the banana, blueberries, yogurt, milk, honey, and ice. Blend on high speed until smooth.

2. If the smoothie is not mixing, add more liquid. If it's too thin, add more ice.

➢ **Beyond the Basics:** I use blueberries and bananas here, but you can use any fruit you like or that is in season. And if you have bananas that are too ripe to eat, don't throw them away—freeze them and use those in your smoothie. You can then use less ice.

Herbed Scrambled Eggs

Even when there's nothing else in the house to eat, chances are you have eggs. Just add a few herbs for a quick and exceptionally tasty breakfast. And for lunch or dinner, you can pair these simple scrambled eggs with the Strawberry, Goat Cheese, and Arugula Salad (page 41).

Serves 2 | Prep time: 5 minutes | Cook time: 5 minutes

TOOLS

Bowl, small

Rubber spatula

Measuring spoons

Nonstick sauté pan
   or skillet

Whisk

INGREDIENTS

2 tablespoons **butter**

4 large **eggs**

2 tablespoons **milk**

1 teaspoon chopped
   fresh **chives**

½ teaspoon dried **thyme**

½ teaspoon **kosher salt**

½ teaspoon freshly ground
   black pepper

1. In a nonstick sauté pan or skillet over medium heat, melt the butter.

2. In a small bowl, whisk the eggs, milk, chives, thyme, salt, and pepper with a whisk until well blended. Pour the eggs into the pan and stir them with a rubber spatula. Cook for about 2 minutes, stirring, until the eggs are firm but still a little glossy, or until your desired doneness.

Bacon Herb Strata

A strata is basically a savory bread pudding. It's a great way to use up slightly stale bread while impressing your dining companions. And it isn't restricted to breakfast. It also makes a great brunch, lunch, or dinner.

Serves 4 | Prep time: 15 minutes | Cook time: 35 minutes

TOOLS

8-by-8-inch baking pan or casserole
Aluminum foil
Bowl, large
Box grater
Chef's knife
Cutting board
Dry measuring cups
Liquid measuring cup
Oven mitts
Serrated knife
Whisk

➤ **Make It Easier:** Steps 1 and 2 can be done the day before and the dish baked the following morning, making it the perfect do-ahead dish. In fact, if you're using slightly stale bread, it really benefits from the extra soak time. Either way, you definitely want to use a bread with texture. A plain white bread will become too mushy.

INGREDIENTS

3 large **eggs**
¾ cup **milk**
½ teaspoon **kosher salt**
½ teaspoon freshly ground **black pepper**
3½ cups **artisan bread cubes** (1 inch)

6 slices **bacon**, cooked and chopped
1 cup grated **Cheddar cheese**
¼ cup chopped fresh **parsley**
2 tablespoons chopped fresh **chives**
1 tablespoon **butter**

1. In a large bowl, whisk the eggs, milk, salt, and pepper with a whisk.

2. Add the bread cubes, bacon, Cheddar cheese, parsley, and chives. Toss the mixture well to coat the bread thoroughly. Cover the bowl and refrigerate for at least 1 hour.

3. Preheat the oven to 350°F.

4. Coat the baking pan with the butter.

5. Pour the egg-bread mixture into the prepared baking pan.

6. Cover the pan with aluminum foil and bake for 30 minutes.

7. Remove the foil and turn the oven to broil. Broil the strata for 5 minutes, or until browned and crunchy on top, keeping an eye out so it doesn't burn.

Apple Berry Dutch Baby

A Dutch baby is an American derivation of a German-style pancake, commonly thought to have been developed in Seattle in the early 1900s. It's believed the name is a result of the cook's daughter mispronouncing the word *Deutsch* (referring to German). Any way you say it, this breakfast dish is magical. The batter seems so innocent. But after just moments in a hot oven, it puffs up to five times its size and turns golden brown. What's not to love?

Serves 4 | Prep time: 15 minutes | Cook time: 30 minutes

TOOLS

Bowl, medium

Cast-iron skillet or heavy ovenproof sauté pan

Chef's knife

Cutting board

Dry measuring cups

Large skillet

Liquid measuring cup

Measuring spoons

Oven mitts

Vegetable peeler

Whisk

INGREDIENTS

For the Dutch baby

1 tablespoon **butter**

3 large **eggs**

¾ cup **milk**

¾ cup **all-purpose flour**

½ teaspoon **kosher salt**

Powdered sugar, for dusting

For the filling

2 **apples**, peeled and thinly sliced

4 tablespoons **butter**, melted

¼ cup **granulated sugar**

1 cup fresh **raspberries**

1 teaspoon ground **cinnamon**

TO MAKE THE DUTCH BABY

1. Preheat the oven to 450°F.

2. Place the butter in a cast-iron skillet and place the skillet in the oven to melt the butter.

3. In the meantime, in a medium bowl, whisk the eggs, milk, flour, and salt with a whisk until smooth and combined.

4. When the butter melts, pour the batter into the skillet and return it to the oven for 15 minutes.

5. Lower the oven temperature to 350°F and bake the Dutch baby for 10 minutes more, or until it is fluffy.

TO MAKE THE FILLING

1. While the pancake bakes, in a large skillet over medium-high heat, combine the apples, melted butter, and granulated sugar. Sauté for about 6 minutes, until soft.

2. Stir in the raspberries and cinnamon. Remove the filling from the heat and set aside.

TO FINISH

1. Slide the Dutch baby out of the skillet onto a cutting board.

2. Pour the filling into the middle of the Dutch baby.

3. Fold the pancake over like an omelet. Sprinkle with powdered sugar and slice to serve.

➤ **Swap It:** Not a fan of apples? Try pears. When peaches are in season, they are delicious as a filling, too.

Orange-Spiced French Toast

Why wait for a special occasion to enjoy French toast? This recipe is delicious any day of the week.

Serves 4 | Prep time: 10 minutes | Cook time: 10 minutes

TOOLS

Bowl, large
Cutting board
Large skillet
Liquid measuring cup
Measuring spoons
Metal fish spatula
Serrated knife
Whisk

INGREDIENTS

½ cup freshly squeezed **orange juice**

⅓ cup **milk**

½ teaspoon ground **cinnamon**

½ teaspoon **vanilla extract**

¼ teaspoon **kosher salt**

3 large **eggs**

3 tablespoons **butter**, plus more as needed

8 (1-inch-thick) slices **French bread**

1 tablespoon **powdered sugar**, for dusting

Syrup of choice, for serving

1. In a large bowl, use a whisk to blend the orange juice, milk, cinnamon, vanilla, salt, and eggs.

2. Place a large skillet over medium-high heat and add the butter to melt.

3. One slice at a time, dip the bread into the egg mixture, turning to coat and letting any excess fall back into the bowl. Place the coated bread in the skillet. Fry for about 4 minutes per side, using a metal fish spatula to flip the bread over, until golden brown. Add more butter to the skillet, if needed.

4. Dust the cooked French toast with powdered sugar and serve with syrup.

Cinnamon Crunch Muffins

Sometimes only a muffin will do. Topped with crunchy cinnamon bits, these baked beauties offer a special surprise inside—more of that delicious cinnamon crunchiness. They're perfect fresh out of the oven with a steaming cup of coffee.

Makes 12 muffins | Prep time: 20 minutes | Cook time: 20 minutes

TOOLS

Bowls, 1 small,
   1 medium, 1 large
Dry measuring cups
Handheld electric mixer or
   stand mixer
Liquid measuring cup
Muffin liners
Muffin tin
Measuring spoons
Oven mitts
Toothpick

INGREDIENTS

For the topping

¾ cup **all-purpose flour**
½ cup packed **light
   brown sugar**
1 teaspoon ground
   cinnamon
½ teaspoon **kosher salt**
4 tablespoons
   butter, melted

For the muffins

2 cups **all-purpose flour**
2 teaspoons
   baking powder
½ teaspoon **kosher salt**
8 tablespoons (1 stick)
   butter, at room
   temperature
1 cup **sugar**
2 large **eggs**
½ cup **milk**
1 teaspoon **vanilla extract**

TO MAKE THE TOPPING

1. In a small bowl, stir together the flour, light brown sugar, cinnamon, and salt.

2. Pour in the melted butter and stir to mix well. Set aside.

CONTINUED

Cinnamon Crunch Muffins CONTINUED

TO MAKE THE MUFFINS

1. Preheat the oven to 375°F. Line a standard muffin tin with muffin liners.

2. In a medium bowl, stir together the flour, baking powder, and salt. Set aside.

3. In a large bowl, using a handheld electric mixer, or in a stand mixer, cream (mix) together the butter and sugar for about 4 minutes, until it is light and fluffy.

4. One at a time, add the eggs, mixing well to incorporate after each addition.

5. Pour in the milk and vanilla and mix thoroughly.

6. Stop the mixer and add the flour mixture. Starting on the lowest speed, blend the ingredients together. The dough will be thick.

7. Using a ¼-cup measure, place 1 scoop of dough in each cup of the prepared muffin tin. Top each scoop with 1 tablespoon of crumb topping. Add a second scoop of batter to each muffin. Top each with an equal amount of the remaining crumb topping, pushing it down onto the batter to adhere.

8. Bake for 20 minutes, or until a toothpick inserted into the center of a muffin comes out clean— with no batter sticking to it.

9. Remove the muffins from the oven and let cool slightly before serving.

▷ **Beyond the Basics:** If you want to make these muffins even more enticing, whip up a quick glaze to drizzle over the top. In a small bowl, whisk 1 cup powdered sugar, 1 tablespoon melted butter, and 2 tablespoons milk. If you feel adventurous, add a splash of vanilla extract.

CHAPTER TEN
Snacks + Small Bites

Apple, Bacon, Brie Flatbread Pizza

Sometimes you just have to have pizza. Nothing else will do. This gourmet version is super quick and so delicious. It also makes a fabulous hors d'oeuvre for your next party. Flatbreads are found in the bread aisle of your favorite grocery store. They can be round (perfect for a single pizza) or rectangular (for a larger group).

Serves 4 | Prep time: 15 minutes | Cook time: 5 minutes

TOOLS

Box grater
Chef's knife
Cutting board
Large sheet pan
Measuring spoons
Metal fish spatula
Oven mitts
Pastry brush

INGREDIENTS

4 small round **flatbreads**

2 tablespoons **extra-virgin olive oil**

2 ounces **Brie cheese**, thinly sliced

2 **Gala apples**, thinly sliced

¼ cup grated **Parmesan cheese**

2 slices **applewood-smoked bacon**, cooked and crumbled

Honey, for drizzling

1. Preheat the broiler.

2. Place the flatbreads on a sheet pan and broil them for 1 minute, or until lightly golden.

3. Remove the flatbreads from the oven, flip them over on the pan, and use a pastry brush to brush them evenly with the olive oil.

4. Top the flatbreads with the Brie, evenly dividing it between them.

5. Arrange the apple slices on top of the Brie.

6. Sprinkle each flatbread with 1 tablespoon of Parmesan cheese and one-quarter of the bacon.

7. Broil the flatbreads for 1 to 2 minutes, or until the Brie melts.

8. Using a metal fish spatula, remove them from the oven and drizzle the flatbreads with honey before serving.

➤ **Swap It:** If you don't have or can't find flatbread, use pizza dough, pitas, or naan instead. They all make great crusts.

Sweet and Spicy Popcorn

If you were a fan of Cracker Jack as a child, you're going to love this adult version. Along with the sweet, buttery flavors, there's a bit of heat. It's the perfect snack for your next movie night.

Serves 4 | Prep time: 5 minutes | Cook time: 10 minutes

TOOLS

Bowl, large
Dry measuring cups
Large pot with lid
Measuring spoons
Oven mitts
Small saucepan
Whisk

INGREDIENTS

For the popcorn

3 tablespoons
   vegetable oil

1 cup **popcorn kernels**

For the topping

4 tablespoons **butter**
¼ cup packed **light
   brown sugar**

1 teaspoon ground
   chipotle pepper
Kosher salt

TO MAKE THE POPCORN

1. Pour the vegetable oil into a large pot, making sure the entire bottom of the pot is coated with the oil.

2. Pour in the popcorn, being careful to cover the entire bottom of the pot with it. Cover the pot with a lid, place the pot on the stove, and turn the heat to high.

3. As the popcorn begins to pop, occasionally shake the pan.

4. For perfect popcorn, turn off the heat when you can count to 3 without hearing any more popping.

5. Remove the lid and transfer the popcorn to a large bowl.

CONTINUED

Sweet and Spicy Popcorn CONTINUED

TO MAKE THE TOPPING

1. In a small saucepan over medium heat, melt the butter.

2. Use a whisk to incorporate the brown sugar and chipotle pepper, whisking until they dissolve.

3. Pour the hot topping over the popcorn and stir well to coat. Season liberally with salt.

➤ **Swap It:** If you're more in the mood for a savory snack, replace the topping with ½ cup freshly grated Parmesan cheese and some salt and black pepper—a take on Cacio e Pepe (page 47).

Trail Mix

Trail mix is one of life's great snacks. Not only is it good for you, but it's also the perfect combination of sweet, salty, and crunchy. Pack a bag and take it with you wherever you go.

Makes 4 cups | Prep time: 5 minutes

TOOLS

Bowl, large

Dry measuring cups

Mason jar or zip-top
  plastic bag

INGREDIENTS

¾ cup toasted **almonds**,
  whole or sliced

¾ cup salted **cashews**

½ cup dried **cranberries**

½ cup **golden raisins**

½ cup salted
  sunflower seeds

½ cup **dark
  chocolate chips**

½ cup sweetened
  shredded **coconut flakes**

In a large bowl, combine the almonds, cashews, cranberries, raisins, sunflower seeds, chocolate chips, and coconut flakes. Toss well to mix. Store at room temperature in a Mason jar or resealable plastic bag.

Swap It: This recipe is just a guideline. Substitute any dried fruit, nut, or seed you prefer. Go ahead and make this one your own.

No-Bake Energy Bites

These treats are the perfect snack when you're craving something sweet but don't want junk food. They're also a great pick-me-up before and after a workout.

Makes 24 bites | Prep time: 10 minutes

TOOLS

Bowl, large

Dry measuring cups

Large sheet pan

Liquid measuring cup

Measuring spoons

Parchment paper

INGREDIENTS

1 cup old-fashioned rolled **oats**

¾ cup sweetened **coconut flakes**

½ cup **peanut butter**, smooth or crunchy

½ cup mini **semisweet chocolate chips**

⅓ cup ground **flaxseed**

⅓ cup **honey**

1 teaspoon **vanilla extract**

1. Line a sheet pan with parchment paper. Set aside.

2. In a large bowl, combine the oats, coconut, peanut butter, chocolate chips, flaxseed, honey, and vanilla. Stir well to mix.

3. Form tablespoon-size portions of dough into balls. Roll each ball in your hands to pack it tightly, and place it on the prepared sheet pan.

4. Refrigerate the energy bites for about 30 minutes before serving.

➤ **Swap It:** If you are allergic to peanut butter, substitute almond butter or any nut or seed butter in this recipe. You can also substitute white chocolate chips or butterscotch chips in place of the chocolate chips for a little variety.

Baked Kale Chips

Kale chips are a healthy snack that you can easily make at home. So, save yourself the high price of store-bought chips. But be warned—you won't be able to eat just one!

Serves 4 | Prep time: 10 minutes | Cook time: 25 minutes

TOOLS

Bowl, large
Chef's knife
Large sheet pan
Measuring spoons
Oven mitts
Parchment paper

INGREDIENTS

½ bunch **kale**, washed, thoroughly dried, stems removed

1 tablespoon **extra-virgin olive oil**

¼ teaspoon **sea salt**

Freshly ground **black pepper**

1. Preheat the oven to 325°F. Line a large sheet pan with parchment paper and set aside.

2. Roughly tear the kale leaves into large pieces and place them in a large bowl.

3. Pour in the olive oil and toss until all the pieces are well-coated with the oil.

4. Sprinkle the salt onto the leaves, season with pepper, and toss well again. Spread the kale on the prepared sheet pan, being sure not to over-crowd it.

5. Bake for 10 minutes. Rotate the pan and bake for 12 to 15 minutes more, or until the kale begins to crisp up. (This usually takes about 25 minutes total.)

6. Enjoy the kale immediately as it does not store well.

➤ **Beyond the Basics:** If you want to add a little more flavor to these chips, head to your spice rack for some cumin, cayenne, smoked paprika, and chili powder, and season to taste. They'll be perfect on these chips.

Guacamole

Guacamole makes a great snack that is not only packed with healthy fats but is so quick to make, especially when you substitute salsa for the traditional chopped onions and tomatoes. Enjoy this with your favorite tortilla chips or on Fresh Fish Tacos (page 151).

Serves 6 | Prep time: 10 minutes

TOOLS

Bowl, medium
Chef's knife
Liquid measuring cup
Potato masher or fork

INGREDIENTS

3 **avocados**
¼ cup tomato-based **salsa**
3 **garlic cloves**, minced
1 teaspoon ground **cumin**
1 teaspoon **kosher salt**
Juice of 1 **lime**
Freshly ground
   black pepper

1. Carefully halve the avocados lengthwise with your chef's knife, stopping at the pit. Twist the two halves in opposite direction to separate them. Remove the pit and scoop the avocado flesh into a medium bowl.

2. Add the salsa, garlic, cumin, salt, and lime juice, and season with pepper. Using a potato masher or fork, mash the mixture until it is as smooth as you like, being careful to incorporate the ingredients fully.

3. Taste and adjust the seasonings, as needed.

CHAPTER ELEVEN
Salads + Veggies

Caprese Salad

When tomatoes are in season, few things are as fresh and delicious as Caprese salad. With a splash of high-quality extra-virgin olive oil and balsamic vinegar, it tastes like being in Italy.

Serves 4 | Prep time: 10 minutes

TOOLS

Chef's knife

Cutting board

Dry measuring cups

INGREDIENTS

2 ripe **tomatoes**, sliced

1 (8-ounce) ball fresh **mozzarella cheese**, sliced

¼ cup torn fresh **basil**

Extra-virgin olive oil, for drizzling

Balsamic vinegar, for drizzling

Sea salt or other finishing salt (see page 76)

Freshly ground **black pepper**

1. On a serving dish or on individual plates, arrange the tomato and mozzarella slices, alternating as you go.

2. Top the salad with the basil.

3. Drizzle with olive oil and vinegar.

4. Season with salt and pepper.

Mexican-Style Street Corn Salad

Introducing the perfect side dish to Fresh Fish Tacos (page 151) or Sheet Pan Fajita Shrimp (page 139). When fresh corn is in season, this salad is at its peak. It calls for crema, a fresh dairy product similar to sour cream that is the traditional base for street corn. It is available in most grocery stores, but you can use a good-quality mayonnaise if you can't find it.

Serves 4 | Prep time: 10 minutes | Cook time: 10 minutes

TOOLS

Can opener
Dry measuring cups
Large sauté pan or skillet
Measuring spoons
Wooden spoon

INGREDIENTS

1 tablespoon **extra-virgin olive oil**

2 (14.5-ounce) cans **sweet corn**, drained, or 2 cups fresh corn kernels

½ cup **Cotija cheese** or feta cheese, crumbled

¼ cup **crema** or mayonnaise

¼ cup chopped fresh **cilantro**

Juice of 1 **lime**

Freshly ground **black pepper**

Kosher salt (optional)

1. In a large sauté pan or skillet over medium-high heat, heat the olive oil until it shimmers and moves easily around the pan.

2. Add the corn and cook for about 5 minutes, until lightly browned. Remove the pan from the heat.

3. Stir in the cheese, crema, cilantro, and lime juice. Season with pepper, then taste and season to taste with salt (if using).

➤ **Beyond the Basics:** Traditional Mexican street corn is made by grilling corn on the cob. If you're feeling adventurous and want to give it a try, simply cut the ends off 2 ears of corn, pull back the husks to remove the silks, and brush each cob with crema. Grill the corn over medium-high heat, turning it regularly until the kernels are soft, about 10 minutes. When cool enough to handle, stand the cobs on their flat ends and carefully cut the kernels off the cob with your chef's knife.

Greek Salad

If you're tired of the same old garden salad, look no further than this classic Greek version. Teeming with fresh grape tomatoes, cucumbers, olives, and dill, it is the perfect summer side dish. Add a few grilled shrimp and it becomes the main meal.

Serves 4 | Prep time: 15 minutes

TOOLS

Bowls, 1 small, 1 large
Chef's knife
Cutting board
Dry measuring cups
Liquid measuring cup
Measuring spoons
Tongs
Whisk

INGREDIENTS

For the dressing

¼ cup **extra-virgin olive oil**

2 tablespoons freshly squeezed **lemon juice**

3 tablespoons chopped fresh **dill**

1 teaspoon dried **oregano**

For the salad

1 large head **romaine lettuce**, rinsed, dried, and roughly chopped into bite-size pieces

1 cup **grape tomatoes**, halved

½ **red onion**, thinly sliced

¼ cup crumbled **feta cheese**

¼ cup Kalamata **olives**, pitted and halved

½ **cucumber**, diced

TO MAKE THE DRESSING

In a small bowl, whisk the olive oil, lemon juice, dill, and oregano with a whisk until well blended. Set aside.

TO MAKE THE SALAD

1. Place the lettuce, tomatoes, red onion, feta cheese, olives, and cucumber in a large bowl.

2. Add the dressing, and toss ingredients with tongs until they are properly coated.

Broccoli-Apple Slaw

Jazz up common coleslaw with a few unexpected ingredients. This is a great way to use up broccoli stems, which are so often thrown away. Use a firm-fleshed apple for this recipe, too—Fuji and Gala are both good choices.

Serves 6 | Prep time: 20 minutes

TOOLS

Bowl, large
Chef's knife
Cutting board
Dry measuring cups
Liquid measuring cup
Measuring spoons
Vegetable peeler

INGREDIENTS

For the dressing

1 cup **mayonnaise**
¼ cup **apple cider vinegar**
¼ cup **sugar**

1 teaspoon **kosher salt**
½ teaspoon freshly ground **black pepper**
½ teaspoon **poppy seeds**

For the slaw

6 **broccoli stems**, peeled, very thinly sliced, and cut into thin strips

1 **apple**, cored, thinly sliced, and cut into thin strips

TO MAKE THE DRESSING

⟋ In a large bowl, stir together the mayonnaise, vinegar, sugar, salt, pepper, and poppy seeds until blended. Set aside.

TO MAKE THE SLAW

⟋ Add the broccoli and apples to the dressing. Toss well to combine.

▷ **Make It Easier:** Cutting the broccoli stems and apples into thin strips can be time-consuming. Consider investing in a simple julienne vegetable peeler. It makes thin strips in one easy pull of the peeler. If you want to make it even easier, pick up a bag of broccoli slaw. Already cut into beautiful thin strips, it can be found with the prewashed, bagged salad greens in your grocer's produce section.

Roasted Sweet Potato Fries

Who doesn't love French fries? This recipe is a twist on classic oven fries and pairs nicely with Cast-Iron Rib Eye Steak (page 61).

Serves 4 | Prep time: 10 minutes | Cook time: 20 minutes

TOOLS

Bowl, medium
Chef's knife
Cutting board
Large sheet pan
Measuring spoons
Metal fish spatula or tongs
Oven mitts
Vegetable peeler

INGREDIENTS

2 large **sweet potatoes**, peeled and cut into French fry-sized pieces
2 tablespoons **extra-virgin olive oil**
Kosher salt
Freshly ground **black pepper**
1 teaspoon **chili powder** (optional)

1. Place a sheet pan in the oven and preheat the oven to 425°F.

2. In a medium bowl, combine the sweet potatoes and olive oil, and season with salt and pepper. Toss until the sweet potato pieces are evenly coated.

3. Carefully spread the sweet potato pieces on the hot sheet pan so they do not touch.

4. Bake for 10 minutes. Using a spatula or tongs, flip the sweet potato pieces over.

5. Roast for 10 minutes more, or until the fries are browned and slightly crunchy.

6. Season with a little more salt and the chili powder (if using).

➤ **Beyond the Basics:** You don't have to preheat the sheet pan in the oven, but if you do, your sweet potato fries will be crispier. This is true for all roasted vegetables. It doesn't take any extra time, and the end result is so much better. It's also important that you don't overcrowd the pan. When the sweet potatoes touch each other or overlap, they will steam rather than roast. If needed, use multiple pans for the best roasted vegetables.

Classic Mashed Potatoes

Few dishes are as comforting as a steaming bowl of creamy mashed potatoes. From Roasted Chicken (page 83) with Chicken Gravy (page 86) to Cast-Iron Rib Eye Steak (page 61), it's the perfect accompaniment for any hearty entrée.

Serves 4 | Prep time: 10 minutes | Cook time: 25 minutes

TOOLS

Chef's knife

Colander

Cutting board

Fork

Handheld electric mixer or potato masher

Large saucepan or pot

Liquid measuring cup

Measuring spoons

Vegetable peeler

INGREDIENTS

3 teaspoons **kosher salt**, divided

4 **russet potatoes** or Yukon Gold potatoes, peeled and quartered

4 tablespoons **butter**, cut into 4 pieces

Freshly ground **black pepper**

⅓ cup **milk** or half-and-half

1. Fill a large saucepan or pot halfway with water and add 1 teaspoon of salt. Place the pan on the stove, cover it, and bring the water to a boil over high heat.

2. Add the potatoes to the boiling water and cook for 12 to 15 minutes, depending on how large your pieces are, until they are fork-tender—meaning a fork inserted into them goes through easily.

3. Turn off the heat and let the potatoes sit in the hot water for 10 minutes.

4. Drain the potatoes into a colander.

5. Return the potatoes to the saucepan on the burner. The residual heat from the burner will evaporate any excess moisture in the potatoes, giving you fluffier mashed potatoes.

6. Add the butter and remaining 2 teaspoons of salt, and season with pepper. Using a handheld electric mixer or a potato masher, break up the potatoes just until they begin to look mashed.

7. Pour in the milk and continue to mix until the potatoes are creamy, light, and fluffy.

➤ **Beyond the Basics:** Russet potatoes—also known as Idaho potatoes—are high in starch and will give the best results in this recipe. Yukon Gold potatoes are another great choice because of their flavor, starch content, and beautiful color. It's also important not to cut the potatoes into small pieces. While smaller ones will cook faster, they will absorb too much moisture and you'll end up with soggy mashed potatoes.

Honey-Glazed Carrots

Carrots, though available year-round, are at their best in winter months. If you can find a heritage variety (multicolored and smaller in size), try them with this recipe. If not, no worries. Regular carrots will work just fine.

Serves 4 | Prep time: 10 minutes | Cook time: 25 minutes

TOOLS

Bowl, large

Chef's knife

Cutting board

Large sheet pan

Liquid measuring cup

Measuring spoons

Oven mitts

Tongs

Vegetable peeler

INGREDIENTS

1 pound **carrots**, peeled and halved lengthwise if thick

2 tablespoons **extra-virgin olive oil**

1 teaspoon **kosher salt**

1 teaspoon freshly ground **black pepper**

¼ cup **honey**

1. Place a large sheet pan in the oven and preheat the oven to 375°F.

2. In a large bowl, toss together the carrots, olive oil, salt, and pepper to combine. Carefully spread the carrots on the hot sheet pan, being careful not to crowd the pan.

3. Roast for 12 minutes.

4. Using tongs, turn the carrots over.

5. Roast for 10 minutes more.

6. Pour the honey over the carrots, tossing to coat them.

7. Roast for 2 minutes more, or until the carrots are tender but not mushy.

Sautéed Brussels Sprouts with Bacon

If you are not a Brussels sprouts lover, give them another try with this recipe. The addition of bacon and Parmesan cheese will make you a believer.

Serves 4 | Prep time: 10 minutes | Cook time: 20 minutes

TOOLS

Chef's knife
Cutting board
Large sauté pan or skillet
Paper towels
Plate
Tongs

INGREDIENTS

5 slices **bacon**
1 pound **Brussels sprouts**, trimmed and very thinly sliced
1 **onion**, diced
Kosher salt
Freshly ground **black pepper**
¼ cup grated **Parmesan cheese**

1. Line a plate with paper towels and set aside.

2. Place the bacon slices in a single, even layer in a cold sauté pan or skillet and place the pan on the stovetop. Turn the heat to medium-high and cook the bacon for 4 to 7 minutes, until it is browned on one side. Using tongs, flip the bacon and cook the other side for 4 to 5 minutes more, until well-browned.

3. Using tongs, transfer the cooked bacon to the prepared plate to drain. When cool, crumble the bacon and set aside.

4. Drain all but 1 tablespoon of bacon fat from the pan and return it to medium-high heat.

5. Add the Brussels sprouts and onion. Lightly season with salt and pepper and cook for 5 minutes, or until they are tender.

6. Turn off the heat and top with the Parmesan cheese and crumbled bacon.

Main Dishes

Pasta Bolognese

Pasta Bolognese is a classic Italian dish with a meat-based sauce, common to and originating from the city of Bologna. Sounds so much more elegant than "pasta with meat sauce," don't you think? No matter what you call it, this is one of life's classic comfort foods. While Bolognese sauce is traditionally served over long, flat noodles called tagliatelle, this recipe uses spaghetti. But feel free to serve it over your favorite pasta shape, paired with a simple salad and bottle of good red wine.

Serves 4 | Prep time: 10 minutes | Cook time: 55 minutes

TOOLS

Can opener
Chef's knife
Colander
Cutting board
Large pot
Liquid measuring cups
Measuring spoons
Medium saucepan with lid

INGREDIENTS

1 pound lean **ground beef**

1 large **onion**, minced

2 **garlic cloves**, minced

1 (28-ounce) can **crushed tomatoes**

5 tablespoons **tomato paste**

½ cup **dry red wine**

1 teaspoon dried **basil**

1 teaspoon dried **oregano**

Kosher salt

Freshly ground **black pepper**

1 pound **spaghetti** (or any type of pasta shape)

1. In a medium saucepan over medium-high heat, brown the ground beef for 5 minutes, stirring occasionally. Remove the beef from the skillet and pour out all but 2 tablespoons of fat.

2. Return the pan to the heat and add the onion. Cook for 5 minutes, until softened and translucent.

3. Add the garlic and cook for 30 seconds.

4. Stir in the tomatoes, tomato paste, red wine, basil, oregano, and cooked beef, and season with salt and pepper. Cover the pan, reduce the heat to maintain a simmer, and cook for 30 minutes, stirring occasionally.

5. Bring a large pot of water to a boil over high heat. Add the spaghetti and stir it immediately so it doesn't stick to the pan or itself. Turn the heat to medium-high and cook the pasta for 9 minutes, or until al dente, stirring occasionally to prevent it from sticking.

6. Drain the pasta into a colander. Do not rinse it.

7. Serve the hot red sauce over the pasta.

▷ **Swap It:** If you're trying to cut down on your fat intake, ground turkey is a great substitute. If you want to add a bit more flavor, use a spicy pork sausage instead, or even a combination of the two.

Blue Cheese and Bacon Burger

Cheeseburgers are an American classic. Instead of using the usual Cheddar, take the flavor up a notch with pungent blue cheese and salty, crunchy bacon. After all, there are few things in life that can't be improved by adding bacon!

Serves 4 | Prep time: 5 minutes | Cook time: 20 minutes

TOOLS

Dry measuring cups

Instant-read thermometer

Large sauté pan or skillet with lid

Metal fish spatula

Paper towels

Plates, 2

Tongs

INGREDIENTS

8 slices **bacon**

1 pound **ground beef**

⅓ cup crumbled **blue cheese**

4 **hamburger buns**

1. Line 2 plates with paper towels and set aside.

2. Place the bacon slices in a single, even layer in a cold sauté pan or skillet on the stovetop. Turn the heat to medium-high and cook the bacon for 4 to 7 minutes, until it is browned on one side. Using tongs, flip the bacon over and cook the other side for 4 to 5 minutes more, until well-browned.

3. Using tongs, transfer the cooked bacon to one of the prepared plates to drain, leaving the fat in the pan. Set the bacon aside.

4. Divide the ground beef into 4 equal portions and shape each into a ½-inch-thick round patty about 5 inches in diameter.

5. Return the pan with the bacon fat to medium-high heat.

6. Add the hamburger patties. Cook for about 4 minutes, flipping them with a metal fish spatula once halfway through the cooking time and using a thermometer to check doneness (see page 17).

CONTINUED

Blue Cheese and Bacon Burger

7. Just before the burgers reach the desired internal temperature, top each with blue cheese. Cover the pan and cook for 1 to 2 minutes, or until the cheese is just melted.

8. Transfer the burgers to the second prepared plate to drain any excess grease.

9. Place the burgers on the buns and top each with 2 slices of bacon.

> **Beyond the Basics:** To prevent your burger from shrinking too much when you cook it, use your thumb to indent the middle of the raw burger before you add it to the pan.

Maple-Roasted Pork Tenderloin with Apples

Pork seems like a Sunday afternoon dish, but if you opt for a tenderloin, dinner can be on the table in less than an hour. Smaller in size than a full loin, this cut makes the perfect weeknight meal. Serve with roasted vegetables or a salad to round out the plate.

Serves 6 | Prep time: 10 minutes | Cook time: 25 minutes

TOOLS

Chef's knife
Cutting board
Instant-read thermometer
Liquid measuring cup
Measuring spoons
Oven mitts
Roasting pan
Whisk

INGREDIENTS

2 (¾-pound) **pork tenderloins**, trimmed of extra fat
1 tablespoon **extra-virgin olive oil**
Kosher salt
Freshly ground **black pepper**
4 **apples**, thickly sliced
¾ cup freshly squeezed **orange juice**
¼ cup pure **maple syrup**
1 teaspoon **cornstarch**

1. Preheat the oven to 375°F.

2. Coat the tenderloins with the olive oil and season with salt and pepper. Place the tenderloins in a roasting pan and position the apples alongside them.

3. Roast for about 20 minutes, or until the pork's internal temperature reaches 145°F on an instant-read thermometer.

4. Meanwhile, in a liquid measuring cup, whisk the orange juice, maple syrup, and cornstarch with a whisk until the cornstarch dissolves. Pour the sauce over the pork and return it to the oven for 5 minutes more.

5. Let the pork rest for 10 minutes before slicing and serving with the apples and sauce from the pan.

Sheet Pan Fajita Shrimp

Sheet pan dinners are the ultimate one-dish meal, and this one is done in record time. Start by roasting the veggies, top them with the shrimp, and you're done in under 30 minutes. Serve with your favorite fajita toppings to round out the meal.

Serves 4 | Prep time: 10 minutes | Cook time: 10 minutes

TOOLS

Bowls, 1 small, 1 large
Chef's knife
Cutting board
Large sheet pan
Measuring spoons
Oven mitts

INGREDIENTS

For the fajita seasoning

2 teaspoons **chili powder**

1 teaspoon ground **cumin**

1 teaspoon **smoked paprika**

1 teaspoon **garlic powder**

½ teaspoon **kosher salt**

½ teaspoon freshly ground **black pepper**

For the shrimp

1 **yellow bell pepper**, cut lengthwise into ¼-inch-thick strips

1 **orange bell pepper**, cut lengthwise into ¼-inch-thick strips

1 large **onion**, sliced

2 tablespoons **extra-virgin olive oil**

1 teaspoon **kosher salt**

½ teaspoon freshly ground **black pepper**

1¼ pounds 21/25 count **shrimp**, peeled and deveined (see Beyond the Basics tip)

8 flour or corn **tortillas**, warmed

TO MAKE THE FAJITA SEASONING

In a small bowl, stir together the chili powder, cumin, paprika, garlic powder, salt, and pepper. Set aside.

TO MAKE THE SHRIMP

1. Place a sheet pan in the oven. Preheat the oven to 450°F.

CONTINUED

2. In a large bowl, combine the yellow and orange bell peppers, onion, olive oil, salt, and pepper. Toss to coat the vegetables in the oil and carefully spread them on the hot sheet pan. Roast for 5 minutes.

3. Add the shrimp to the sheet pan and toss well to coat. Roast for 4 minutes.

4. Serve with the warmed tortillas—and any toppings you like.

▷ **Beyond the Basics:** If you haven't bought the shrimp already peeled and deveined, you can learn to do so yourself: To peel the shrimp, remove the tough outer shell and discard it. To devein the shrimp, using a paring knife, cut along the entire top length of the shrimp, about ¼ inch deep, and remove the dark vein. Rinse the shrimp before using.

▷ **Swap It:** Shrimp makes a super-quick weeknight meal, but substitute chicken strips if you prefer. Just know they will take 12 to 15 minutes longer to cook.

Teriyaki Salmon Rice Bowl with Edamame

All-in-one bowls make dinner and the resulting cleanup a breeze. It doesn't hurt that this one, in particular, is extremely delicious. Shelled edamame (otherwise known as soybeans) are available in most frozen-food aisles and add a good punch of soy protein to this dish.

Serves 2 | Prep time: 10 minutes | Cook time: 20 minutes

TOOLS

Bowl, small
Chef's knife
Cutting board
Dry measuring cups
Large sheet pan
Liquid measuring cup
Measuring spoons
Metal fish spatula
Parchment paper
Small saucepan with lid

INGREDIENTS

1 cup **water**

½ cup **brown rice**

1 cup small **broccoli florets**

¼ cup shelled **edamame**

1 **onion**, quartered

2 (4- to 6-ounce) **salmon fillets**

2 tablespoons **extra-virgin olive oil**

2 **garlic cloves**, minced

½ cup **teriyaki sauce**

1 teaspoon toasted **sesame seeds**

1. In a small saucepan, bring the water to a boil over high. Pour in the rice and stir. Cover the pan, reduce the heat to low, and cook for 20 minutes, or until the rice is softened.

2. Preheat the broiler. Line a sheet pan with parchment paper.

3. Place the broccoli, edamame, onion, and salmon on the prepared sheet pan. Drizzle the vegetables and fish with the olive oil.

4. Broil for 8 to 10 minutes, or until the fish is firm to the touch and cooked through. If it still feels squishy, it needs to cook a bit more until firm.

5. In a small bowl, stir together the garlic and teriyaki sauce. Pour the sauce over the fish and broil for 1 minute.

6. Place some rice in the bottom of two bowls. Top each with a piece of salmon and some veggies. Garnish with the sesame seeds.

Garlic and Tomato Steamed Mussels

Make sure you eat this with a great crusty bread. You'll want to soak up all those amazing juices from the bowl. If you want to bulk up this recipe a little, add a spicy sausage along with the garlic and tomatoes. Just make sure the sausage is cooked through before you add the mussels, as they cook very quickly.

Serves 4 | Prep time: 5 minutes | Cook time: 10 minutes

TOOLS

Can opener
Chef's knife
Cutting board
Dry measuring cups
Large spoon
Large stockpot with lid
Liquid measuring cup
Measuring spoons

INGREDIENTS

3 pounds **mussels**, rinsed, scrubbed, and debearded (see Beyond the Basics tip)

1½ tablespoons **extra-virgin olive oil**

1 tablespoon **butter**

3 medium **garlic cloves**, finely chopped

1 (14.5-ounce) can **diced tomatoes**, drained

¼ teaspoon **red pepper flakes**

½ cup **dry white wine**

4 tablespoons chopped fresh **flat-leaf parsley**, divided

1. In a large stockpot over medium heat, combine the olive oil and butter, and heat until the butter melts.

2. Stir in the garlic, tomatoes, and red pepper flakes. Cook for 2 minutes.

3. Add the mussels, white wine, and 2 tablespoons of parsley.

4. Increase the heat to high and cover the pot. Cook for 2 minutes.

5. Remove the lid and toss the mussels well with a large spoon. Re-cover the pot and cook for 3 to 4 minutes more until the mussels have opened wide. Discard any mussels that have not opened.

6. Divide the mussels between 4 bowls. Pour the broth over the top and garnish with the remaining 2 tablespoons of parsley.

➤ **Beyond the Basics:** To prep the mussels, place them in a large bowl and cover them with cold water. Examine each mussel to be sure it closes completely. Pull off any beards or scrubby dark brown hairs on the outside of the mussel. Throw away the beards and any mussels that are cracked or don't fully close.

Beef and Broccoli Stir-Fry

Who needs takeout when you have this recipe? It can be done and on the table before a delivery person could even get to your door. Feel free to use a less expensive cut than the steak suggested here. Just know it will be tougher, due to the cut and the cooking method.

Serves 4 | Prep time: 10 minutes | Cook time: 20 minutes

TOOLS

Chef's knife

Cutting board

Dry measuring cups

Large sauté pan or skillet

Large spoon

Liquid measuring cup

Measuring spoons

Small saucepan with lid

Tongs

Vegetable peeler

Whisk

INGREDIENTS

4½ cups **water**, divided

2 cups **rice**

2 tablespoons **vegetable oil**

1½ pounds **rib eye steak** or New York strip steak, thinly sliced

Kosher salt

Freshly ground **black pepper**

4 cups **broccoli florets**

1 **onion**, sliced

½ cup reduced-sodium **soy sauce**

2 tablespoons **light brown sugar**

3 tablespoons **cornstarch**

1½ teaspoons grated peeled fresh **ginger**

3 **garlic cloves**, minced

1 teaspoon **red pepper flakes**

1. In a small saucepan, bring 4 cups of water to a boil over high heat. Pour in the rice and stir. Cover the pan, reduce the heat to low, and cook for 20 minutes, or until the rice is softened.

2. After the rice has been cooking for 10 minutes, in a large sauté pan or skillet over medium-high heat, heat the vegetable oil until it moves easily around the pan.

3. Season the steak slices with salt and pepper. Add them to the pan and sauté for about 2 minutes per side, using tongs to flip them, until browned. Remove the steak from the pan and set aside.

CONTINUED

4. Return the skillet to the heat and add the broccoli and onion. Sauté for about 4 minutes until softened.

5. Meanwhile, in a liquid measuring cup, use a whisk to whisk the soy sauce, remaining ½ cup of water, brown sugar, cornstarch, ginger, garlic, and red pepper flakes until the cornstarch dissolves.

6. Once the vegetables are softened, return the steak to the pan.

7. Pour the sauce over the veggies and beef and cook, stirring, until the sauce thickens.

8. Taste and adjust the seasonings, if needed.

9. Spoon the cooked rice onto plates and top with the beef and broccoli.

> **Make It Easier:** Looking to get dinner on the table even quicker? Grab your veggies already cut from the salad bar at your local grocery store and cut your prep time in half!

Pan-Seared Chicken with Rustic Mustard Sauce

This dish is so elegant and packed with flavor. You don't need to tell anyone how easy it is to prepare. Serve it with Steamed Broccoli Parmesan (page 51) for a complete meal.

Serves 4 | Prep time: 5 minutes | Cook time: 15 minutes

TOOLS

Bowls, 2 small

Chef's knife

Cutting board

Dry measuring cups

Instant-read thermometer

Large skillet

Measuring spoons

Tongs

Whisk or fork

INGREDIENTS

For the chicken

1 tablespoon whole-grain **Dijon mustard**

2 tablespoons **extra-virgin olive oil**, divided

2 teaspoons minced fresh **rosemary**

4 boneless, skinless **chicken breasts**

1 teaspoon **kosher salt**

1 teaspoon freshly ground **black pepper**

For the sauce

2 tablespoons whole-grain **Dijon mustard**

½ cup **sour cream**

1 tablespoon freshly squeezed **lemon juice**

2 tablespoons **water**

TO MAKE THE CHICKEN

1. In a small bowl, stir together the mustard, 1 tablespoon of olive oil, and the rosemary. Spread the mustard mixture over both sides of the chicken breasts. Season the chicken with salt and pepper.

2. Place a large skillet over medium-high heat, and add the remaining tablespoon of olive oil.

CONTINUED

Pan-Seared Chicken with Rustic Mustard Sauce CONTINUED

3. When the oil is hot, add the chicken breasts and pan-sear until they are nicely browned, 4 to 5 minutes per side, and cooked all the way through to an internal temperature of 165°F on an instant-read thermometer.

TO MAKE THE SAUCE

1. While the chicken cooks, in another small bowl, use a whisk or fork to stir together the mustard, sour cream, lemon juice, and water, mixing well.

2. Serve the sauce over the cooked chicken.

➤ **Swap It:** Can't find fresh rosemary? Dried will do. Use ¾ teaspoon and soak it in the olive oil so it doesn't burn while you're cooking the chicken.

Fresh Fish Tacos

Want to take a virtual vacation? Whip up these fresh fish tacos for dinner. Spread out an array of toppings and let your guests go wild.

Serves 4 | Prep time: 15 minutes | Cook time: 10 minutes

TOOLS

Bowl, small
Chef's knife
Cutting board
Dry measuring cups
Large sheet pan
Measuring spoons
Parchment paper

INGREDIENTS

½ teaspoon dried **oregano**
½ teaspoon dried **thyme**
¼ teaspoon **smoked paprika**
⅛ teaspoon ground **cayenne pepper**
¼ teaspoon freshly ground **black pepper**
½ teaspoon **kosher salt**
4 **tilapia fillets**

1½ tablespoons **extra-virgin olive oil**
8 flour or corn **tortillas**, warmed
2 cups shredded **cabbage**
½ cup **sour cream**
½ cup **salsa**
2 **avocados**, diced
1 **lime**, cut into wedges

1. In a small bowl, stir together the oregano, thyme, paprika, cayenne, black pepper, and salt.

2. Preheat the broiler and position a rack as close to the broiler element as possible. Line a sheet pan with parchment paper.

3. Rub each fish fillet with the olive oil followed by the seasoning mix. Place the fillets on the prepared sheet pan.

4. Broil the fish for about 6 minutes until it is firm and cooked through. If it still feels squishy, it needs to cook a bit longer until firm. Serve the fish in the warmed tortillas along with the cabbage, sour cream, salsa, avocados, and lime.

➤ **Swap It:** I use tilapia here because it's thin, cooks quickly, and is widely available. But any fish will do. Just note that a thicker fish will take longer to cook.

Desserts

Affogato with Almond Biscotti

Affogato sounds fancy, but it is one of the easiest and most delicious desserts you can make. It literally means "drowned" in Italian, and it's made by pouring a shot of espresso (and amaretto, if you're looking for an extra after-dinner kick) over vanilla ice cream or gelato. In this recipe, we're pairing it with another Italian treat: biscotti.

Serves 4 | Prep time: 15 minutes | Cook time: 1 hour 5 minutes

TOOLS

Bowls, 1 medium, 1 large

Cutting board

Dry measuring cups

Handheld electric mixer or stand mixer

Large baking sheet

Measuring spoons

Oven mitts

Parchment paper

Serrated knife

Wire cooling rack

INGREDIENTS

For the biscotti

2¼ cups **all-purpose flour**, plus more for dusting

2 teaspoons **baking powder**

½ teaspoon **kosher salt**

5 tablespoons unsalted **butter**, at room temperature

1 cup **sugar**

2 large **eggs**

1 teaspoon **almond extract**

½ teaspoon **vanilla extract**

1 cup whole **unsalted almonds**

For the affogato

1 pint **vanilla ice cream** or gelato

2 shots **espresso** or strongly brewed coffee

TO MAKE THE BISCOTTI

1. Preheat the oven to 350°F. Line a baking sheet with parchment paper.

2. In a medium bowl, stir together the flour, baking powder, and salt. Set aside.

3. In a large bowl, using a handheld electric mixer, or in a stand mixer, cream (mix) together the butter and sugar until light and fluffy.

4. Add the eggs, almond extract, and vanilla to the butter mixture and continue to mix until well blended.

5. With the mixer on low speed, pour in the flour mixture and beat until just incorporated. Gently stir in the almonds.

6. Dust your hands well with flour and divide the dough in half. Shape each half into a 3-by-12-inch log.

7. Place the logs on the prepared baking sheet, leaving room between them so they won't touch when they bake.

8. Bake for 25 minutes, or until the logs have puffed up and are somewhat firm.

9. Remove from the oven and let the logs cool for 10 minutes. Transfer the logs to a cutting board.

10. Reduce the oven temperature to 250°F.

11. Using a serrated knife, cut the logs on an angle into 1-inch-thick slices. Place the pieces, cut-side down, on the baking sheet and return it to the oven for 20 minutes.

12. Flip the biscotti over and bake for 20 minutes more, or until they are golden brown and crunchy. Transfer the biscotti to a wire rack to cool completely.

TO MAKE THE AFFOGATO

Scoop the ice cream into a serving dish. Pour the espresso over the top and serve with biscotti on top.

Make it Easier: Rather not bake your own biscotti? Head to the cookie aisle at your local grocery store and pick up a bag. Nonni's is a nationwide brand that produces a delicious biscotti.

Chocolate-Chipotle Brownies

These fudgy brownies are the perfect combination of sweet, smoky, and spicy. Adjust the amount of chipotle to suit your heat tolerance.

Makes 12 brownies | Prep time: 15 minutes | Cook time: 30 minutes

TOOLS

8-by-8-inch baking pan
Bowl, large
Dry measuring cups
Measuring spoons
Medium saucepan
Oven mitts
Parchment paper
Rubber spatula
Whisk
Wire cooling rack

INGREDIENTS

Nonstick cooking spray

12 tablespoons (1½ sticks) **butter**

½ cup **cocoa powder**

1¼ cups packed **light brown sugar**

1 large **egg**, whisked

¾ cup **all-purpose flour**

1 teaspoon **baking powder**

1 teaspoon ground **cinnamon**

½ teaspoon **kosher salt**

½ teaspoon ground **chipotle pepper**

1 teaspoon **vanilla extract**

1. Preheat the oven to 350°F. Spray an 8-by-8-inch square baking pan with cooking spray and line the pan with parchment paper. Set aside.

2. In a medium saucepan over medium heat, melt the butter. Remove the pan from the heat and whisk in the cocoa powder and brown sugar.

3. Whisk in the egg.

4. In a large bowl, stir together the flour, baking powder, cinnamon, salt, and chipotle pepper. Whisk the dry ingredients into the chocolate mixture, combining well.

5. Whisk in the vanilla. Use a rubber spatula to scrape the batter into the prepared baking pan.

6. Bake for 25 minutes.

7. Let the brownies cool on a wire rack for about 10 minutes. Remove the brownies from the pan by pulling up the parchment paper. Slice and serve.

➤ **Make It Easier:** Brownies can be tough to cut. They stick to even the sharpest metal knives. An easy way around this is to use a plastic knife. It will cut right through, and the brownies won't stick to it.

Chocolate-Drizzled Coconut Macaroons

These pantry-friendly cookies require just four ingredients and come together in no time. If you chose to sprinkle a handful of toasted almonds on top, they're just like eating a candy bar.

Makes 10 cookies | Prep time: 10 minutes | Cook time: 15 minutes

TOOLS

Bowls, 1 small microwave-
    able, 1 large
Cookie scoop
Dry measuring cups
Large sheet pan
Measuring spoons
Oven mitts
Parchment paper
Rubber spatula

INGREDIENTS

2 cups sweetened
    coconut flakes
2 large **egg whites**
½ teaspoon **almond
    extract** or vanilla extract
2 ounces **semisweet
    chocolate**
¼ cup chopped toasted
    almonds (optional)

1. Preheat the oven to 350°F. Line a sheet pan with parchment paper and set aside.

2. In a large bowl, stir together the coconut, egg whites, and almond extract.

3. Using a cookie scoop, form the dough into balls and place them on the prepared sheet pan about 1 inch apart.

4. Bake for 15 minutes, or until browned.

5. Remove the macaroons from the oven and let cool.

6. In a small microwaveable bowl, gently melt the chocolate in the microwave for 30 seconds. Using a rubber spatula, stir and heat for 30 seconds more, if needed.

7. Dip half of each cookie into the melted chocolate, or drizzle with the chocolate, and return the cookies to the parchment paper.

8. Garnish with the chopped almonds (if using) and let cool.

   ➤ **Beyond the Basics:** Toasting nuts is so easy and adds incredible flavor to your cookies. To toast them, simply place the dry almonds in a sauté pan or skillet over medium heat. Shake the nuts around in the pan occasionally until they begin to turn brown. Remove from the heat and you're done.

Best-Ever Oatmeal-Cranberry Cookies

Who doesn't love an old-fashioned oatmeal cookie? In this version, we replace the classic raisins with tart and sweet dried cranberries. You're going to love them.

Makes 24 cookies | Prep time: 15 minutes | Cook time: 15 minutes

TOOLS

Bowls, 2 small, 1 large
Cookie scoop
Dry measuring cups
Handheld electric mixer or stand mixer
Large baking sheet
Measuring spoons
Metal fish spatula
Oven mitts
Parchment paper
Wire cooling rack

INGREDIENTS

8 tablespoons (1 stick) **butter**, at room temperature
½ cup **granulated sugar**
½ cup packed **light brown sugar**
1 large **egg**
¾ teaspoon **vanilla extract**

1 cup **all-purpose flour**
½ teaspoon **baking powder**
½ teaspoon **baking soda**
¼ teaspoon **kosher salt**
1 cup old-fashioned rolled **oats**
½ cup dried **cranberries**

1. Preheat the oven to 350°F. Line a baking sheet with parchment paper and set aside.

2. In a large bowl, using a handheld electric mixer, or in a stand mixer, cream (mix) together the butter, granulated sugar, and brown sugar until well blended and light and fluffy.

3. Add the egg and mix well until incorporated. Pour in the vanilla and blend again thoroughly.

4. In a small bowl, stir together the flour, baking powder, baking soda, and salt.

5. In another small bowl, combine the oats and cranberries.

CONTINUED

6. Add the flour mixture to the butter mixture and mix well, starting on low speed, to combine.

7. Add the oatmeal and cranberries, mixing well (use a wooden spoon if the batter is too stiff).

8. Using a cookie scoop, form dough balls and place them on the prepared baking sheet about 1 inch apart.

9. Bake for about 13 minutes, or until golden brown.

10. Remove from the oven and let the cookies cool slightly.

11. Using a spatula, transfer the cookies to a wire rack to cool completely. Store in an airtight container at room temperature for about 1 week.

➤ **Swap It:** If you prefer chocolate, add ½ cup chocolate chips to the batter instead of the cranberries.

Making More or Less

Sometimes a recipe makes way more than you need. Other times, it's not enough. That's when you have to do a little math.

For example, a recipe says it serves 2 people, but you are having 4 guests for dinner. In this instance, you're going to need to double the recipe. To do that, simply multiply each ingredient by 2. If the recipe calls for 1 cup of milk, you will need 2 cups of milk. Continue to do this with each ingredient, with the exception of bold herbs and spices, in which case you should use 1½ times the amount (page 79).

If the recipe says it serves 4 people but there will only be 2 of you for dinner, halve the recipe, or divide every ingredient by 2. For example, if the recipe calls for 1 cup of flour, you will need only ½ cup of flour. Continue to do this with each ingredient.

I find it helpful to write these new amounts next to the old so you don't forget and accidently put in too much or too little.

Weights + Volume Conversion Table

VOLUME EQUIVALENTS (LIQUID)

US Standard	US Standard (ounces)	Metric (approximate)
2 tablespoons	1 fl. oz.	30 mL
¼ cup	2 fl. oz.	60 mL
½ cup	4 fl. oz.	120 mL
1 cup	8 fl. oz.	240 mL
1½ cups	12 fl. oz.	355 mL
2 cups or 1 pint	16 fl. oz.	475 mL
4 cups or 1 quart	32 fl. oz.	1 L
1 gallon	128 fl. oz.	4 L

OVEN TEMPERATURES

Fahrenheit (F)	Celsius (C) (approximate)
250°F	120°C
300°F	150°C
325°F	165°C
350°F	180°C
375°F	190°C
400°F	200°C
425°F	220°C
450°F	230°C

VOLUME EQUIVALENTS (DRY)

US Standard	Metric (approximate)
⅛ teaspoon	0.5 mL
¼ teaspoon	1 mL
½ teaspoon	2 mL
¾ teaspoon	4 mL
1 teaspoon	5 mL
1 tablespoon	15 mL
¼ cup	59 mL
⅓ cup	79 mL
½ cup	118 mL
⅔ cup	156 mL
¾ cup	177 mL
1 cup	235 mL
2 cups or 1 pint	475 mL
3 cups	700 mL
4 cups or 1 quart	1 L

WEIGHT EQUIVALENTS

US Standard	Metric (approximate)
½ ounce	15 g
1 ounce	30 g
2 ounces	60 g
4 ounces	115 g
8 ounces	225 g
12 ounces	340 g
16 ounces or 1 pound	455 g

Recipe Title Index

Index

Acknowledgments

None of this would have been possible without the love and support of my family. Thank you, Donald, Mom, and Dad. You mean the world to me. And to the amazing women cooks in my life who are no longer with us but who taught me so much—Mommom, Grandma, Andy, and Gertie: Your love, influence, memories, and great recipes live on in this book and every day at No Thyme to Cook.

Huge thanks to my amazing friends Rhonda Rivera and Samantha Boyd for lending their expert editing eyes to the words on these pages. Love you ladies.

And to my entire team at No Thyme to Cook for keeping the place running beautifully while I was writing: Kim Bradbury, Brian Grabarek, Elisabeth Langmack, Bonnie McGraw, Jenni Nargiz, Lauren Woytowitz, Dan Mumbert, Emma Albright, Hanah Albright, Julia Denton, Alexa Grabarek, Brandon House, Alyssa Osburn, and Annice Mattingly-Weaver. You are the best team I could ever ask for. Thank you for all you do.

About the Author

Gwyn Novak is a professional chef and cooking instructor. She owns and operates No Thyme to Cook, a cooking school on Solomons Island in southern Maryland, 90 minutes south of Washington, D.C. A graduate of Bucknell University and the Baltimore International Culinary College, Gwyn has been cooking and writing about food for more than 25 years. Throughout her career, she has been a personal chef and professional caterer, but her passion is teaching others how to prepare simple, delicious meals using locally sourced ingredients.